SPELL JAR BOOK FOR BEGINNERS

SPELL JAR BOOK FOR BEGINNERS

60 ENCHANTING SPELLS TO FOCUS YOUR POWER AND UNLEASH THE MAGIC

PAIGE VANDERBECK

ILLUSTRATIONS BY STUDIO MUTI

ROCKRIDGE
PRESS

Copyright © 2022 by Rockridge Press

First Rockridge Press trade paperback edition 2022

Rockridge Press and the Rockridge Press logo are trademarks or registered trademarks of Callisto Media Inc. and/or its affiliates in the United States and other countries and may not be used without written permission.

For general information on our other products and services, please contact our Customer Care Department within the United States at (866) 744-2665, or outside the United States at (510) 253-0500.

Paperback ISBN: 978-1-68539-018-1
eBook ISBN: 978-1-68539-218-5

Manufactured in the United States of America

Interior and Cover Designer: Karmen Lizzul
Art Producer: Hannah Dickerson
Editor: Katherine De Chant
Production Editor: Matthew Burnett
Production Manager: Holly Haydash

Illustrations © 2022 Studio Muti, except for the following used under license from The Noun Project: pp. 3, 25, 31, 39, 41, 47, 56, 58, 65, 72, 75, 83, 87, 99, 122, 126, 135, 137, 140.

10 9 8 7 6 5 4 3 2 1 0

CONTENTS

INTRODUCTION

The most famous spell jar in history isn't even known to be a jar, but a box—Pandora's box. According to Greek mythology, humans were created by the Olympians, but Zeus didn't teach humans how to survive. Because of this, humans suffered greatly, hunted by predators and dying of starvation. The god Prometheus took pity on us, stole fire from Mount Olympus, and brought it down to the lowly humans. Zeus was livid with Prometheus for helping us, and Prometheus was severely punished for eternity. Zeus also had a special punishment for humanity, which was said to consist only of men at this point. According to the most well-known version of the story, Zeus punished mankind by creating a woman—Pandora.

Pandora was created to be beautiful, intelligent, curious, and willful. All of these qualities were unappreciated in ancient Greek society. Zeus gave Pandora an earthenware jar—box was a mistranslation—and told her she could never open it or see what was inside. Curiosity got the best of Pandora, and she opened the jar, unleashing evil, pestilence, pain, and sadness into the world. She quickly tried to close it back up, not realizing the only thing left inside was hope. Pandora is often framed as a *punishment* for humanity, but there is a different way to interpret this story.

Pandora and her jar didn't curse humanity, she made us whole. Pandora's jar was filled with all the things humans feel and experience. The more unpleasant parts of being alive are also the price we pay for moments of happiness, love, and hope. No matter how you tell it, our very humanity is said to originally come from a magic spell contained in a jar.

These days, the ingredients and intentions behind spell jars are more defined. Spell jars can be used for healing, attracting prosperity, accomplishing goals, and even exploring abstract themes like love and hope. Spell jars allow you to take the intangible, the magical, and the emotional and make them real. Spell jars put the power to change your life, and the lives of others, into your own hands. Armed with only your natural curiosity and a single jar, you can craft an entire world of magic.

My name is Paige Vanderbeck, and I have been a practicing witch since I was nine years old. When I started out, my materials were extremely limited. I relied on things I could find around the house, such as bottles from the recycling bin and spices from the kitchen. In the park, I collected pretty rocks and leaves for my spell work. These commonplace items were my first magical tools and materials. Many years later, I still find much inspiration in the shapes and designs of thrifted glass pieces and pottery.

My love of art, color, and exploration predates my spiritual practice, but it has informed it every step of the way. I have always been interested in creative ways of practicing my craft, so I was instantly drawn in by the versatility and beauty of spell jars. I never feel limited in what I can do with spell jars, and I hope that this book opens a world of possibilities for you, too. Creative energy is pure magic.

Come on, my witchy friend, let's go craft some magic.

HOW TO USE THIS BOOK

This book is divided into two parts—first we'll explore the origins of spell jars and the reasons why they are still so popular among modern witches. Then you'll have the chance to make your way through 60 different spells, rituals, and recipes that can be put to use in every area of your life. You will start to personalize your spells by observing moon phases and astrological seasons, harvesting local flora, and gathering significant mementos. You will discover how to work with the unique magic of your corner of the world. Every jar we build together will be tailored to fit your style and beliefs and grant you access to the life of your dreams.

The spells in this book come in many different forms. Some are potions, meant to be opened up and used, and other spells work best if they stay tightly sealed. Bear in mind that the casting of a spell does not start once the planning, design, and assembly of the spell is complete. It begins as soon as you start the process, using your innate power to connect to the spirits of nature and the universe. Every step is an expression of your spirit and an act of magical devotion to the earth.

This book was written for witches of all skill levels and backgrounds, so you won't find information about worshipping deities or following any particular religious path. Witchcraft isn't always a religion in and of itself but is a set of practices that can help you walk any spiritual path. If you're a true beginner to witchcraft, you'll learn the basics of magical practice and symbolism. If you're a seasoned practitioner of witchcraft who's new to working with spell jars, you'll get a new perspective on an old type of magic. No matter where you are in your journey, congratulations on embarking on a new path.

When you reach the end of the book, you'll find resources to help you continue your studies in spell jars, witch bottles, and other kinds of accessible magic that can help anyone craft a compassionate and fulfilling spiritual practice.

PART I

THE ENCHANTING WORLD OF SPELL JARS

In part 1 we'll explore the history and origins of spell jars, how they're used, and the tools needed to craft them. Though ingredients and methods are important, they're not the whole story. We're going to look at *why* you would work this particular type of spell and how it can infuse your everyday life with magic.

CHAPTER ONE

Spell Jars 101

· ·

efore we move on to amassing tools, gathering ingredients, and casting spells, let's cover the basics. The creation of spell jars and bottles is an ancient practice. When you dive into the history, you will see exactly why this versatile tool is still so popular with modern witches. The possibilities are endless, the benefits are far-reaching, and the magic you can produce is enormously powerful.

What Is a Spell Jar?

A spell jar is, quite simply, a jar containing the ingredients and energy for a specific magic spell. This type of magic falls under the heading of container or vessel spells, which use ordinary objects like boxes, bags, envelopes, bottles, and jars. These containers are turned into magical artifacts as we fill them with ingredients that range from mundane to strange. Charm bags, paper packets, spirit boxes, and a cauldron full of ingredients can be considered container spells, but we're going to focus on a specific type—spell jars.

Also called witch bottles, spell jars are just as popular now as they were in ancient Egypt, Mesopotamia, pre-Christian Europe, and South America before colonization. If you search social media like Instagram and Pinterest, you'll find hundreds of spell jars filled with a huge variety of ingredients, all prepared in different ways. There is no right or wrong way to work container magic, but knowing where it came from and how it evolved can help you craft effective spell jars with respect for the cultures and beliefs that birthed them.

The Origins of Spell Jars

Jars were first created in ancient Mesopotamia, the oldest human civilization that we know of, and their magical uses originated there, too. The first use of spell jars and bottles was protection, and the favored material for this kind of jar was glass made with cobalt to produce a vibrant blue color. Blue was considered a spiritual color in Mesopotamia, the Mediterranean, Egypt, and other parts of the African continent because blue contains the colors of both the sea and sky. As such, it was believed to exist in both the physical and spiritual world—perfect for magic. To make a protection amulet, a spell or prayer was written on a small roll of parchment and placed in a blue glass bottle. Such bottles were hung in windows, in tombs, and on jewelry.

In Central Africa bottles of all colors, but especially blue, were hung on trees to distract or collect evil spirits before they could enter the home. This tradition came to North America with the transatlantic slave trade, and "Bottle Trees" are still a common sight throughout the Southern and Appalachian United States.

In Europe, witch bottles, balls, and jars were made with clear glass and featured a wide range of ingredients that included salt, iron nails and pins, broken glass, dirt, personal concerns (hair, urine, blood), wine, and botanicals. Unlike Africa's sparkling blue trees, witch bottles were often buried in the ground, kept in dark cupboards, or hidden in walls and under floorboards. In general, magic and spirituality from western Europe tends to feature a strong element of secrecy—like the belief that you can't reveal the wish you make on your birthday cake because it won't come true. European-style witch bottles are still created today, and they are often one of the first magical curios created by new witches.

In the "new world," European, African, Arabic, and Indigenous traditions all contributed to North American folk magic practices, one of which is Hoodoo. Hoodoo is not always classified as a religion, but rather a system of working magic. It was created by Africans who were enslaved and brought to the southern United States, and it was kept a secret from enslavers. Hoodoo uses ingredients that are available in stores or can be made by the practitioner and have magical symbolism or spiritual energy (see the Be Respectful When Practicing Spell Work sidebar on page 18).

A TOOL FOR ALL WITCHES

The fact that jars are a very common household item is part of what makes them so magical. Anyone can create magic with this method, regardless of how much money you have, where you live, or your age. As you read the book, keep in mind that you can always make substitutions for ingredients that are hard to find or inaccessible to you. I live in Canada and come from a Mediterranean background, so I use a lot of recycled pasta sauce jars, rosemary, maple syrup, and olive oil. You may find you use a lot of clay pottery, cactus spines and agave, or volcanic sand. I personally believe that magic is at its best when a witch is crafty with their resources. Every spell jar begins the same way—empty. No matter which ingredients you use, every jar ends up filled with magic.

The Benefits of Spell Jars

A love spell is a love spell no matter how you cast it, but the method can make a difference. Casting a love spell with a candle attracts a fiery, passionate, and physical love experience, but that same spell takes on a gentler, more emotional energy if centered around a magical bath. When that love spell is cast with a jar, it has a strong unifying energy that can attract a love that is emotionally, physically, and spiritually fulfilling all at once. Tapping into their distinctive energetic quality is just one of the many benefits of spell jars.

Tap into Your Personal Power

Although the tools and ingredients used to create a spell jar come from your environment, the magic ultimately comes from you. A jar full of herbs and rocks doesn't become magic until someone like you decides to make it so. With every step of the process, you put a little bit of yourself into the spell. Your intention or wish is what brings it to life. Everyone has their own power, but we live in a world where many people have to fight and work hard to gain control over their lives. This makes many of us feel powerless. You can make spell jars to gain confidence, strength, or protection. Every jar you make allows you to harness your own power.

Embrace a Nourishing Ritual

There's just nothing quite as magical is getting your hands dirty and creating something from nothing. This is ingrained in our DNA, a primal feeling from the earliest incarnations of humanity. Working with our hands has been shown to reduce stress and anxiety, and we receive great satisfaction when we see our creations through to the end. This process boosts self-esteem, flooding the physical and magical body with happy energy. Including handicrafts of any kind in your regular routine can have a positive effect on your mental well-being. Add magic into the mix, and you can create an empowering ritual with positive effects on your spiritual well-being.

Experiment with Magic

Many people think science and witchcraft are incompatible. Fortunately, they're totally wrong. I often apply a modified scientific method to my spell craft. First I determine what I want to accomplish with the spell, then I hypothesize about the kinds of elements and ingredients I could use to magically make that happen. I put all the pieces together, leave them to do their work, and observe what comes next. I take notes, draw conclusions, and decide later if my spell was a success or not. If it wasn't successful, I consider what I could do differently next time and start to form a new hypothesis. Certain containers, like test tubes and bell jars, even carry the energy of curiosity and experimentation in their very design.

Serve the Planet

Almost all the jars I use for magic are recycled or purchased from thrift and antique shops, and they all get washed, cleansed, and reused for as long as possible. When they are no longer usable, the glass and metal can be recycled again. Taking care of the planet is the first step of creating a meaningful relationship with the natural world, and spell jars facilitate this multiple times over.

Most jars are specifically made to preserve whatever is inside. Using them to keep your herbs, oils, and powders fresh will ensure that those natural materials don't go to waste. They also protect the outside world from what you put inside, which could be shards of glass, nails and screws, or even poisonous plants. They keep your spells out of the mouths of animals, slow the filling of landfills, and help you explore the natural world with reverence and mirth.

Get Creative

Every step in the process of crafting a spell jar provides an opportunity to get creative. The size, shape, and color of the jar are carefully chosen to match your purposes. The ingredients are selected for their magical properties, but you can also factor in how they fit together creatively and aesthetically. Some spell jars are meant to be hidden so they can complete their work in peace, and others are meant to be displayed and affect us visually as well as spiritually. You can even add your own decorations to the jar with paint, glue, paper, labels, wax, and anything else you can imagine.

Container spells are also a sensual experience, meaning they engage all your senses. As long as it's safe, you can smell, touch, and taste the ingredients. Employ the magic of sound by selecting ingredients and jars for the noise they make when shaken. Your spell jar can be a magical and beautiful work of art.

Spell Jars Can Enhance Your Life

Witches in movies can snap their fingers and make something appear out of thin air. They benefit by getting something they want, instantly, without much effort. Real magic requires much more effort, and in turn you reap greater rewards. Every method of spell casting has its own unique energy that can have a positive effect on us even if it doesn't come to fruition. The energy of spell jars mirrors that of the cobalt blue glass in ancient times—they provide a place where the spiritual and material can safely come together. Every jar or bottle spell completes this circuit between the heavens, the earth, and you. Container magic allows you to make changes in yourself, in the world around you, and in your relationship with the divine.

Self-Care and Healing

Practicing self-care means prioritizing your feelings and well-being and making time to do the things that make you feel happy, healthy, nourished, and well cared for. Some acts of self-care are basic, like getting enough sleep at night, creating a daily routine, and eating in ways that make you feel good and strong. Other acts of self-care are meant to help you get as much pleasure out of life as possible. Neither type is more important or worthwhile than the other. Magical self-care has all the same goals, with the added focus on spiritual energy and fulfillment. Spells for restful sleep may include magical materials to help banish nightmares or increase the frequency of prophetic dreams. This is often referred to as "holistic" healing, as it works on the whole issue—physically, emotionally, and spiritually.

Abundance and Prosperity

Money magic falls into a few categories—abundance, prosperity, and drawing in. Money drawing spells are used to bring in extra money when cold, hard cash is the answer to your problem. Prosperity spells help ensure that your job or business will prosper or be successful, which includes bringing in good money. Abundance magic is not specifically money based, but instead it focuses on having a full life where you always have what you need and enough to share. Mason jars are especially appropriate for abundance spells because of their history in food preservation, which has the potential to save a lot of money.

Inspiration and Motivation

An empty jar begs to be filled, and a jar full of magical ingredients begs for your attention. Spell jars made to inspire and motivate are beautiful, visual, and impossible to ignore. They are often experimental, demanding creativity and innovation: a small jar of magical blackberry ink here, a spelled candy jar to create a positive work environment there. Not only will you be able to find the inspiration and motivation you need for your original purpose, but the act of creating these jars will inspire you to cast more spells with all-new combinations and designs. Sounds like a win-win situation to me.

Boundaries and Protection

One specific subject we won't be covering in this book is "baneful" magic, which includes things like cursing others, getting revenge, and causing destruction. There's nothing wrong with this type of magic—in fact, these spells are often cast by people who have been oppressed, abused, or are in a desperate situation. But baneful magic uses ingredients and methods that don't translate as well to other areas. Instead, we'll focus on magic to help you stay (and feel) safe; set magical, physical, and emotional boundaries; and confidently navigate challenging situations. My hope is that these protective spells, along with those in the self-care and healing chapter, will give you tools to help you get justice, cultivate resilience, and even help others in the future.

Relationships and Romance

When it comes to love and relationships, spell jars are the perfect tool because they bring unique ingredients together to form something new and beautiful. They allow you to look beyond what makes these things different and see instead how they complement each other, how they can work together toward a common goal. Love is the magic we make when we connect with each other on a spiritual level, and that is exactly what happens with the ingredients in your spell jar.

Caring for Your Home

Jars are, first and foremost, domestic objects. They were made to be used around the home, to help us harvest the fruits of the earth, and to provide for our families. With their connections to magic for both protection and abundance, spell jars can make your current home feel safe and nourishing or help you find a new one. A jar that includes your favorite herbs and spices can magically invoke some inspiration while you cook or help you infuse every dish with love. The container serves as a proxy for your home. As you fill it with intentions and ingredients, you fill your home with magic.

Connecting with the Natural World

Botanicals and crystals are the main ingredients in most spell jars and witch bottles. These natural materials are incredibly powerful, and, even more important, they afford us opportunities to get up close and personal with nature. Communing with nature is proven to reduce stress and make us feel calmer overall. The weight of a sparkling crystal in your hand is grounding, the smell of aromatic oils is exhilarating, and the feeling of fresh flower petals on your skin makes you feel beautiful and loved. As you care for the earth by recycling and reusing, the earth lends its magical energy to support your spells and intentions.

Navigating Daily Life

Spell jars are such a versatile tool that they can be used for aid and guidance in any situation. They can be made simply and quickly for a pressing matter, or, alternatively, filled with complex ingredients and kept for years to achieve larger goals. Small jars and bottles can be made into portable spells that you carry in your purse or hang on a chain around your neck. Make one for your desk to help you get that promotion or for your car to make sure you never get lost. Once you get the hang of crafting magical containers, you can adapt the spells and rituals in this book to fit seamlessly into your magical life.

PUT PEN TO PAPER

As a writer, journaling and note-taking have always been a part of my witchcraft practice. Keeping a record of your spells, ingredients, experimentations, and results is a great way to stay organized, but even I know it can be challenging to get into this habit. If scientific documentation isn't your forte, journaling can also provide a safe place for you to explore your goals and intentions. This helps you focus your energy and tap into your spell work more deeply. I find writing by hand helps me focus and reduces my anxiety, but you can choose to type on a laptop, dictate into your phone, or even film yourself. Keep it private or share it with the world. It's your choice and there is no wrong one.

Embrace the Power Within

When combined with the energy of your own intentions, creativity, and curiosity, a simple jar can become a vessel for powerful magic. As you collect your supplies and ingredients in the coming chapter, remember that most of the energy that powers your spell comes from you. You, like the botanicals and crystals you'll encounter in the next chapter, are a part of the natural world and thus the world of magic. The power you seek lives inside you—all you have to do is open up and let it out.

CHAPTER TWO

Ready Your Spell Jar Tool Kit

• • • • • • • • • • • • • • • • • • • •

ow that you know the history and benefits of working with container magic, it's time to collect your tools and find natural allies. The energy and symbolism of your spell is influenced by many factors, including the type of bottle or jar, colors, botanicals, crystals, and curios you use. Each decision contributes to the energy and symbolism of your spell and gives you a chance to make a meaningful connection with the universe.

Gather Your Materials

If you are the power that drives your spell, think of the ingredients in your jar as friends or allies who want to help you succeed. With their different talents and traits, they all contribute something to the work. You can cast spells with nothing but willpower, but being able to ask for help is a sign of strength and character. Accepting help encourages growth and reinforces our relationships. When we ask for help in the art of witchcraft, we strengthen our relationship with the earth.

As you build up your magical stockpile, consider the environmental impacts of your selections. Contrary to popular belief, you don't need expensive stones or exotic herbs to cast spells. If you have access to those items and an ethical supplier, enjoy your magical sampling of magic from around the world. If not, explore the natural environment of where you are. River rocks and beach glass can work like crystals, sand can stand in for salt, and pine cones and acorns have just as much power as the majestic trees they fall from. Even shed whiskers and fur from your beloved pet have their place in magic.

The process of selecting tools and ingredients is just as creative as the act of putting them all together, so allow yourself to explore and experiment with the help of these magical allies.

Jars Come in All Shapes and Sizes

The jar in the story of Pandora served a few purposes. Not only did it hold all the ingredients needed, but it was also made of clay, serving to conceal the contents and increase Pandora's curiosity. It also had a lid that could easily be opened, which sent the energy of those ingredients out in search of their target. The shape, size, material, and color of your jars can lend unique energy to your spells. Using clear glass instead of blue or a tall jar instead of a short one won't get in the way of your magic, but it can help reinforce the symbolism and energy of the jar's contents.

The most common container you'll be using for spell jars will be canning jars, which we also call mason jars, after their original creator, John Landis Mason. This is the most universal and accessible container for spell jars because they have a dual lid system that creates a hermetic seal and is interchangeable across brands and even sizes of jar. Some spell jars need to be airtight, but oftentimes you can have some fun with cork stoppers, fabric, or wax. Mason jars have a wide enough mouth that larger crystals, botanicals, and sticks can all fit and be removed. Bottlenecks are better for smaller items that aren't likely to get stuck.

Jar Shapes

Associated elements are in parentheses.

Cylinder (all elements): All-purpose. A classic jar or bottle is neutral; it can be used for any spell or intention.

Heart (water): Love, beauty, sensuality, healing, relationships, and romance.

Hexagon (water): Keeping secrets, the unknown, natural beauty, love, mystique. Hexagonal jars are often used to hold honey, so they make beautiful honey jars (page 93).

Pyramid (aether): Psychic power, knowledge, the divine, ingenuity, and upward mobility. This shape sends your intentions and energy upward, which can be used for communicating with the divine or "moving up" in the world.

Sphere (water): Connection, magic, safety, circle of life, global reach, and planetary magic. Small jars and bottles with spherical bodies and skinny necks are potion bottles—according to films and fairy tales, anyway. If they have cork stoppers, all the better.

Square (earth): Stability, home, prosperity, abundance, safety, setting boundaries, and starting new projects.

Star (all elements): Protection, elemental magic, getting noticed, fame, astrology, and pleasure.

Material

Earthenware materials such as clay and ceramic have a deep, earthy energy, and they keep your spell a secret because they're opaque. As the most ancient material for containers, they also help you connect to ancestors and the past. Glass is the most common material for spell jars and is completely multipurpose, though no less earthy or beautiful.

If you only have plastic or resin jars or bottles on hand, you can still make magic with them, although there are limits to what you can do. These materials are not biodegradable, but reusing plastic bottles and jars instead of sending them to a landfill *is* a service to the planet.

Jar Color

We'll talk more about colors later in the chapter, but colored glass serves mundane as well as magical purposes.

Amber (brown): Abundance, stability, safety. Amber glass helps filter out sunlight, which can damage herbs, essential oils, and even some crystals.

Clear: Clarity, truth, exposure, beauty. Clear glass is neutral, but consider whether your spell should (or shouldn't) be seen inside the jar.

Cobalt blue: Spiritual protection, psychic power, intuition, emotion, countering the evil eye.

Green: Preservation, growth, prosperity, money. Green glass filters out less sunlight than amber but still prevents the contents from oxidizing.

Purple: Ancient wisdom, magic, spirituality, ancestors, innovation. Manganese lilac purple is the first color humans ever added to glass.

These next two colors of glass don't have many established uses in witchcraft, but they provide some interesting opportunities. Associated elements and planets are in parentheses.

Ultraviolet/black (fire, Saturn): Protection, innovation, setting boundaries, curiosity. This new type of glass filters out only the visible light rays that cause damage, allowing infrared light to reach what's inside and act as a preservative.

Uranium glass (air, Uranus): Childhood innocence, curiosity, truth seeking, defusing negative emotions like greed, bitterness, and jealousy ("seeing green"). Sometimes called "Depression glass," this type of vintage glass contains uranium that makes it fluoresce brilliantly under ultraviolet light. Although uranium is radioactive, the amount of radioactivity is considered negligible and harmless to humans.

Botanicals, Seasonings, and Tea Leaves

Using botanicals in your spell work is a beautiful way to connect to the power of nature. Botanicals include herbs, plants, seeds, spices, wood, leaves, and flowers, and they can be fresh or dried. In spell jars, botanicals can be burned as incense, steeped in water for tea and baths, made into ink or paint, and infused in oil. You can find amazing plants from all over the world at witch shops and new age shops, herbalists, farmers' markets, and even in your own kitchen cupboard. Coffee, cinnamon, and rosemary are all powerful additions to spell jars and witch bottles. Associated elements and planets are in parentheses.

Blue cornflower (air, Venus): Communication, defusing arguments, psychic power, forgiveness, reconciliation.

Chamomile (water, Sun): Good luck, sleep, health, peace, prosperity.

Cinnamon (fire, Sun): Passion, attraction, money, good luck, creativity, humor.

Coffee (air/earth, Uranus): Mental clarity, speed, divination, eliminating obstacles, grounding, revolution.

Mugwort (earth, Moon): Witchcraft, psychic power, dream magic, cleansing, healing, safe travel.

Rose (water, Venus): Spirituality, purification, love, the heart, beauty, emotional healing, romance.

Rosemary (air, Moon): Remembrance, cleansing, ancestors, home, wisdom.

Salt and pepper (earth/fire, Moon/Mars): Cleansing, purification, banishing, protection, grounding.

Tea (water/fire, Moon/Mars): Healing, peace, intellect, clarity, courage, prosperity, vitality.

BE RESPECTFUL WHEN PRACTICING SPELL WORK

Some of the most widely recognized forms of witchcraft are associated with the British Isles, but modern witchcraft has developed out of an extensive range of cultural influences. Some witchcraft practices use meditation techniques and chakra points from Hinduism, burning white sage, sacred in some North American Indigenous traditions, and crafting honey jars, a staple of the African American tradition Hoodoo.

Cultural appropriation is an important dynamic to be aware of when practicing spell work. In witchcraft, cultural appropriation often occurs when someone uses a practice from a culture they are not a part of without getting permission from the people who created it. It may look like selling your own version of someone else's tradition for profit, distorting the practice into something else, or proclaiming yourself an expert in the practice. Any of these behaviors, no matter how good the intentions, can result in pain and hurt toward the people of the originating culture, as well as perpetuation of existing racist dynamics.

None of this means you have to limit your spiritual exploration to the culture or race of your direct ancestors. It means we must all be diligent about checking our own behaviors and how they affect the cultures we are interacting with. For example, many American Indigenous advocates have spoken out against the widespread use of white sage, asking non-Natives to stop using it. Hoodoo witches have also commented on the appropriation of their tradition, which developed to protect enslaved Africans from harm (see References on page 148).

A good place to start is to listen to and learn from witches and advocates from cultures other than your own. Approach practices from cultures that are not your own with honor and respect and accept that you are a guest until informed otherwise.

Essential Oils

Essential oils are also made from botanicals and resins. They can be used in the same way you would use their source material, but these oils have the added benefit of being incredibly aromatic. They can be added to perfumes, potions, and baths or mixed with a carrier like olive oil to create a ritual blend. Essential oils are very concentrated, which is how they got their name. So with only a few drops, you can add a lot of your chosen botanical's essence to your spell. Associated elements and planets are in parentheses.

Cedar (fire, Sun): Purification, protection, regrowth, wisdom, balance, empowerment.

Frankincense (air/fire, Sun): Purification, divine assistance, meditation, happiness, satisfaction, spirituality, magic.

Geranium (water, Venus): Happiness, balance, acceptance, decision-making, poise.

Grapefruit (air, Venus): Happiness, emotional balance, focus, self-esteem, beauty, love, intuition.

Jasmine (water, Moon/Neptune): Sensuality, sexuality, love, abundance, divination, dream magic, intuition, beauty.

Lavender (air, Mercury): Relaxation, spiritual cleansing, balance, mental clarity, healing, divination, reconciliation.

Patchouli (earth, Saturn): Attraction, pleasure, luxury, fertility, sensuality, grounding, growth.

Sage (air/earth, Jupiter): Wisdom, cleansing, blessing, protection, grounding, mental clarity, spirituality.

Sandalwood (water, Moon): Intuition, psychic power, love, enlightenment, sensuality, meditation.

Essential oils are photosensitive, so keep them out of sunlight in the amber bottles they come in. This photosensitivity also makes them potentially harmful if applied to the skin undiluted, so exercise caution when wearing them outside.

Candles and Colors

Candles are one of the most-used tools in any kind of spell, and container spells are no exception. Some spells in this book specifically call for chime candles, which are tapered candles that come in a variety of colors and often burn all the way down in a single sitting. However, you can use many different types of candles to cleanse space, release energy, and attract the attention of the universe. Candle wax can also be used to seal up spell jars and invoke the magic of color. Every color is tied to the elements, planets, astrological signs, emotions, and different types of magical energy.

Black and white (all elements, Moon): Multipurpose, protection, spirituality, cleansing, healing (w), banishing (b), full moon (w), new moon (b).

Brown (earth, Earth): Stability, foundation, animal healing, the law, family.

Dark blue (water, Jupiter): Psychic power, intuition, vision, wisdom, emotional healing.

Green (earth, Jupiter): Abundance, money, healing, compassion, growth, starting anew, fertility.

Light blue (air, Mercury): Communication, healing, peace, authenticity, truth.

Orange (fire, Venus): Attraction, creativity, inspiration, enthusiasm, breaking barriers.

Pink (water, Venus): Love, healing, self-care, the heart, sweetness, childhood.

Purple (aether, Moon): Spirituality, witchcraft, psychic power, success, mastery.

Red (fire, Mars): Passion, love, sex, anger, action, physical energy.

Yellow (air, Sun): Happiness, life, illumination, persuasion, confidence.

Color magic has applications beyond working with candles, and these energetic signatures can be applied to everything from the container itself to the ingredients and adornments you include.

Stones, Crystals, and Gems

All crystals carry the ancient magic of the earth element inside them, which adds a prosperous, safe, and grounding energy to any spell. The stones also have their own unique properties and natural energies that can help support your intentions and other ingredients. Associated elements and planets are in parentheses.

Clear quartz (aether, Sun): Absorbing natural energy, new beginnings, proxy for any crystal.

Garnet (fire, Mars): Protection, passion, will power, resilience, pleasure.

Hematite (earth, Mars): Grounding, vitality, the law, courage, success-drawing.

Honey calcite (fire/air, Jupiter): Abundance, inspiration, growth, nourishment.

Jade (earth, Venus): Good luck, attraction, money, health, longevity, protecting children.

Labradorite (water, Uranus): New moon magic, independence, clairvoyance, truth.

Purple fluorite (air, Neptune): Wisdom, meditation, calming, truth, protection.

Rainbow moonstone (water, Moon): Full moon magic, dreams, safe travel, women's empowerment, emotional healing.

Rose quartz (water, Venus): Friendship, love, beauty, peace.

Sunstone (fire, Sun): Creativity, personal power, sexuality, dispelling fear, talent, independence.

When choosing crystals for your spell, you should also consider their size, shape, and level of polish. Large raw crystals and stones might break if you try to fit them into a bottle, and tumbled crystal chips work perfectly for a smaller container.

INGREDIENTS FOR ADDITIONAL MAGIC

Ingredients like gems and botanicals invoke the power of nature to aid in your spell casting, and the following items help you personalize and adorn your spells. For example, incense can be used to cleanse the energy of your vessel and get you into a meditative state of mind. A lock of hair or photo can tell your spell who to target, and a business card in a spell to find a new job can narrow the focus to a particular company.

- Business cards and signatures
- Carrier oils (olive, jojoba, sweet almond, etc.) and vitamin E
- Charms and talismans
- Droppers and funnels
- Glue
- Incense (sticks/cones, powders, or resins) and fireproof dishes
- Items that belonged to or represent a person (lock of hair, favorite T-shirt, birthstones)
- Lighters or matches
- Metallic mica powder (instead of plastic glitter)
- Mortar and pestle or herb grinder
- Paper and pens, brushes and paints
- Photos

Your Ingredients Are Only as Powerful as You Make Them

Coffee may feel like a magic potion first thing in the morning, but until you purposefully connect with the energy of the coffee beans and channel it for a specific purpose, that coffee only *tastes* magical. As you practice working with magical ingredients and crafting spell jars, you'll notice when you're making a deep connection with nature. You may feel a crystal get warm when you touch it, notice that it shines brighter in your hands, or experience a feeling of calm wash over you whenever you get near it. These are signs that you and your natural allies are on the same wavelength and that their innate magic is mixing with your own, just waiting for you to use it.

CHAPTER THREE

Prepare for Magic

• •

Symbolism and energy are just as important as the physical ingredients you put inside your jars. In this chapter you'll learn about the elements, astrological signs, and moon phases. Practice meditating and begin the task of carving out time and space for your spiritual exploration.

Consider Your Space, Your Ingredients, and Yourself

The amount of preparation you'll need to do will depend on the size and complexity of your spell, but there are a few basic things you can do to ensure you have a safe and enjoyable experience. What matters most is that you feel comfortable and supported in your efforts, so if some of my advice doesn't work for you, I encourage you to discard it and follow your intuition.

Start with a Clean Slate

Before you begin any spell work, clean and dry your tools, containers, hands, and workspace. Spell jars that are meant to be sealed up must be dried thoroughly and, if possible, disinfected before use. This is especially true for recycled jars. Trust me, mold growing in what was a beautiful spell jar ruins the whole vibe.

Clear away clutter that has the potential to get in your way or distract you from your task, and wipe down your surface to get rid of dust or dirt. With the exception of containers and crystals, I don't reuse spell ingredients for another purpose. Every time I cast a spell, I light a new candle and a new stick of incense and fetch new herbs from the shelf. This prevents physical and spiritual cross-contamination.

Get Organized

When it comes to spell work, my system of organization came from a bit of an unlikely source—Martha Stewart. I figure out what kinds of tools and ingredients might be useful for my purposes and then I set up a little workstation in the most convenient place. If I need water I work in the kitchen; if I need access to my clothes I set up on my dresser. I take out my ingredients and lay them out so I can see them all, right next to my notes, which I write out like a recipe. I smell, feel, and measure my ingredients as I go, allowing my intuition to make adjustments if needed. This allows me to stay focused on the spiritual aspect of my spell, rather than getting distracted by the actual assembly.

Cleanse Your Space and Tools

Cleaning refers to washing off debris or germs, and *cleansing* means clearing away spiritual energy or entities from an object, place, or person. You can cleanse energy by wafting smoke from incense like frankincense or sage, spraying salt water, or playing music. It's good to cleanse if you're using something that hasn't been used in a long time, something that triggers intense emotions, or something new. You don't need to cleanse your tools every time you work with them, but cleansing will keep any errant energy from interfering with your spell. The same goes for your home or space. I follow up my weekly cleaning with a cleansing, which leaves my home feeling cozy and safe.

Ground Your Body

Grounding is a calming and meditative practice that helps you focus on the present moment, connect with your body, and invoke feelings of safety and stability. It also helps you connect to the planet and the elements.

Try this basic grounding meditation: Sit or stand comfortably so your hands or feet are flat on the ground. Close your eyes and take four deep breaths. Imagine a beautiful breeze blowing by your face and through your hair, clearing your mind. This is air, the element of intellect. Bring your attention to your heart and listen to your heart beating, pumping warm blood through your body. This is fire, the element of action. Shift your focus to your stomach, where you nourish your body and experience the pangs of emotion and intuition. This is water, the element of feeling. Finally, focus on the solid ground beneath you. The earth element is still and supportive, allowing you to relax in a safe environment. Take four deep breaths and open your eyes.

Focus Your Mind

If you cast a spell with the TV on in the background and a dog nipping at your heels for a walk, your focus is divided. This means you're channeling less energy into your spell. Mindfulness meditation teaches you to quiet racing thoughts and helps keep your focus on the present moment.

Before you cast a spell, try out this simple mindfulness meditation: Sit or lie down comfortably and close your eyes. Put one hand on your stomach and breathe in deeply. Feel your belly fill with air, then breathe out and feel your stomach fall. Continue breathing in and out, focusing on the sound of your breath and the feeling of air moving in and out of your stomach. If you notice your thoughts have wandered, that's okay, just bring your focus back to your breathing. When you're ready, open your eyes and turn your attention to your spell.

Clarify Your Goals and Intentions

What you want from a spell and what you actually need from a spell are not always the same, so take a few minutes to write out your intention and ask yourself a few questions before you get started.

- Why do I want this? Why do I need this?

- What outcome do I expect?

- What is currently standing in my way?

- How can magic make a difference?

If you have tarot or oracle cards, pull them out and ask for a little guidance from the universe and your own intuition.

CENTERING YOUR MIND

Meditation is a skill. The world's best meditators often spend many years learning how—so don't feel bad if you struggle with this practice. Try these techniques if you need a little help.

Walking meditation: Walk along a trail or track at any speed, breathing in time with your footsteps. If you have a clear path, your body can work on releasing physical energy while your mind works through restless thoughts.

Find something to focus on: Light a candle and concentrate on the flame, or burn a stick of incense with a smell you can't get enough of. Relaxing music can also help you practice focusing your attention, and singing or chanting can clear your mind of everything but the sound.

Align Your Spell Work with the Natural World

Time is not a human invention—it was created by nature. Calendars were invented by humans to follow the phases of the moon and movement of the sun across the sky. Seasons change the weather to let us know where we are in our orbit, and the rising and setting of the sun tell us when we move from nighttime to daytime. The movements of planets and stars have been used since humanity's earliest days to communicate with the natural world beyond the horizon. Use the guides below to find the most auspicious times and seasons to cast your spells. Find ways to invoke the energy of the earth and cosmos with magical symbols, colors, and ideas.

The Phases of the Moon

Everyone loves a full moon, especially witches. There's no wrong way to spend or celebrate this beautiful night the universe treats us to every month. Some witches use the magical energy in the air to practice divination or cast powerful spells, and others spend the full moon relaxing, dancing, and stargazing.

Full: Celebration, healing, spiritual development.

Waning: Banishing, letting go, cleansing.

New: Attraction, new projects, emotional development.

Waxing: Inspiration, building, growth.

Special phases like blue moons and lunar eclipses add an extra layer to the energy of the moon. Blue moons help seemingly impossible dreams become possible, and an eclipse shakes things up to kick-start transformation.

The Seasons

Although we don't all experience them the same way, the earth rotates through four seasons in a year, triggered by our relationship with the sun. Each season has an associated element (in parentheses) and an underlying theme. Use symbolism to channel these energies into your spell work.

Spring (air): Renewal, fertility, planting new seeds.

Summer (fire): Action, energy, adventure.

Autumn (water): Togetherness, harvest, mystery.

Winter (earth): Rest, endings, introspection.

This doesn't mean you can only cast fiery spells in the summer. It means that summertime imagery, colors, and botanicals will invoke that active energy any time of year. Trust me, my jar full of sand and shells from the beach keeps me warm through the cold, wet Canadian winters. What are the symbols of the seasons where you live?

Astrological Events

As the earth rotates on its axis and around the sun, we get different views of the stars that surround us. When astrologers say the sun is "in Cancer" it means the sun is in the same part of the sky as the constellation Cancer (or it was, in ancient Mesopotamia). We move through twelve astrological seasons, each of which bears some of the energy of the sign and planet that rule it.

The moon moves through each zodiac sign every two and a half days. Combining the moon's phase with the sign gives you a clear picture of the kind of magical energy available to you. A new moon in Capricorn, for example, is a great time to attract a new job or start a new money-making venture.

The Signs and Planets

Zodiac signs represent planets, ideas, elements, energies, times, and people. Use the symbols and traits in the chart on p. 31 to invoke the power of a planet or sign.

SYMBOL	ZODIAC SIGN	DATE RANGE	PLANET	ELEMENT	IDEA OR ENERGY	COLOR
♈	ARIES	MARCH 21 TO APRIL 19	MARS	FIRE	ACTION	RED
♉	TAURUS	APRIL 20 TO MAY 20	VENUS	EARTH	SENSUALITY	GREEN
♊	GEMINI	MAY 21 TO JUNE 20	MERCURY	AIR	ELOQUENCE	LIGHT BLUE
♋	CANCER	JUNE 21 TO JULY 22	THE MOON	WATER	SENSITIVITY	WHITE
♌	LEO	JULY 23 TO AUGUST 22	THE SUN	FIRE	GLAMOUR	GOLD
♍	VIRGO	AUGUST 23 TO SEPTEMBER 22	MERCURY	EARTH	SERVICE	SLATE GREY
♎	LIBRA	SEPTEMBER 23 TO OCTOBER 22	VENUS	AIR	RELATIONSHIPS	PINK
♏	SCORPIO	OCTOBER 23 TO NOVEMBER 21	PLUTO	WATER	SHADOWS	BLACK
♐	SAGITTARIUS	NOVEMBER 22 TO DECEMBER 21	JUPITER	FIRE	ADVENTURE	NAVY BLUE
♑	CAPRICORN	DECEMBER 22 TO JANUARY 20	SATURN	EARTH	ACHIEVEMENT	FOREST GREEN
♒	AQUARIUS	JANUARY 21 TO FEBRUARY 18	URANUS	AIR	REVOLUTION	LAVENDER
♓	PISCES	FEBRUARY 19 TO MARCH 20	NEPTUNE	WATER	DREAMS	TURQUOISE

The Elements

The magical elements are the building blocks of life in our universe. All seasons, herbs, crystals, colors, stars, planets, and beyond resonate with at least one element. People also have the energy of the elements inside us, which you can feel through grounding and meditation.

Aether—spirit, the universe, magic; light and meditation.

Air—intellect, communication, innovation; smoke and music.

Earth—stability, abundance, sensuality; botanicals and minerals.

Fire—passion, creativity, action; candles and movement.

Water—emotions, intuition, mystery; divination and water.

Aether is not a physical element; it's symbolic and spiritual. The ancient Greeks believed aether was the material of the heavens—the color of the night sky and stars. It's found in beams of light, the sound of prayer, and moments of deep connection. Aether is the element of magic, and though you can't see it, it will be a part of every spell you cast.

Cherish Your Jars

Assembling your jar is just one part of the process. You also have to consider what you'll do with the jar once it's made and how long you plan to keep it. The general rule of thumb is to dismantle your spell once you see results or feel the spell is no longer needed. Jars for long-term magic are frequently sealed and can be kept for as long as the ingredients last inside. Home protection bottles are often permanently sealed and kept for as long as the witch occupies the house. Small bottles and jars that are meant to be carried or worn should also be sealed tight to keep your ingredients safe and yourself safe from your ingredients.

Some jars are made to be hidden, and others are works of art that are meant to be seen. Choose containers that accentuate the aesthetic of your spell and display them in the place they are most needed. A money jar would work best in the office, and a jar for self-esteem or beauty can be displayed on your vanity. The appearance of these spells is important, so be diligent about keeping them clear of dust, out of direct sunlight, and unobstructed by mundane items. If you find that you can't remember to keep up a spell jar and it's sitting neglected, it's time to let it go.

DISPOSING OF YOUR SPELL JAR REMAINS

I generally don't reuse spell ingredients for something else, but jars and bottles are the exception to this rule. When my spell is finished, I usually dismantle it by removing the ingredients and washing out the jar, whether I am reusing it or not. When it comes to disposing of the contents of spell jars, I say "when in doubt, throw it out." There's nothing disrespectful about disposing of spell ingredients in the trash or recycling bins. Sometimes it's the most responsible option. If your ingredients are biodegradable and won't do harm to the environment, you can return them to the earth by burying them in the garden. Be aware that you should never bury things like photographs or glitter because they will not decompose. In any case, I always thank my ingredients for their aid and energy as part of my disposal ritual and give my recycled jars a good cleansing before using them for something new.

Stay Open to the Possibilities

Whether you're trying to attract love, break out of an artistic rut, or align your routine with the phases of the moon, container magic provides you with endless possibilities and clear benefits beyond the bounds of your spell. As you move on to part 2—the spells and rituals—allow yourself room to experiment and improve over time. It's called magical *practice* for a reason. The more spells you cast, the more confident you will be in your ability to make real changes using magical energy. Keep your mind and heart open to the infinite possibilities and spiritual benefits of this ancient, magical art form. Most important, have fun!

PART II

THE MAGIC OF SPELL JARS

Ahead you'll find a whole grimoire's worth of spells for healing, prosperity, love, protection, and spiritual growth. You'll learn how to craft beautiful jars that require a wide variety of ingredients, both common and extraordinary. Even though I've crafted and tested these spells, that only means they work for me. Experiment to learn which spells work best for you. Through this process, you can begin to find your personal style of witchcraft. All these spells can be within your reach, even if you are missing ingredients. Your unique personal touches and substitutions will make your spellwork even more powerful.

CHAPTER FOUR

Spells for Self-Care and Healing

● ●

If Pandora's jar had unleashed nothing but hope, love, and happiness, we would live in a perfect world. In reality, the world we live in is far from perfect. Still, humans can't help but strive for perfection in an imperfect world, and this can lead to damage and pain. We want to be the perfect partners, friends, family members, and employees— even at the expense of our physical, emotional, and spiritual well-being. Self-care is a philosophy that encourages us to focus on our own health and happiness without feeling selfish. To paraphrase Audre Lorde: Self-care is not self-indulgence, it is self-preservation. The spells in this chapter are meant to support you through good times and bad. As you practice these spells, you will be reminded that hope is never as far away as it may seem.

True Love Comes from Within

The best way to care for yourself is to love yourself. For some reason, this is much easier said than done. Feeling unloved and unlovable can sour even the happiest times. This spell employs the heart-healing energy of rose quartz to remind you that the love you seek can always be found within.

Clear mason jar

Water

Pink salt

Knife or small heart-shaped cookie cutter

Peel of a lemon

Sugar

Paper and pen

Rose petals

Rose quartz crystal

Candle

1. Start by cleansing the energy of your jar: Fill the jar ¼ full with water and add a pinch of pink salt. Swirl the salt water around the inside of the jar, then pour some on your hands and wipe the outside of the jar as well. Rinse the jar inside and out with hot water, then set it aside to dry.

2. Using a knife or cookie cutter, cut as many hearts out of your lemon peel as possible. Discard the leftovers.

3. Once the jar has dried completely, sprinkle a thin layer of pink salt on the bottom of the jar. This cleanses away self-doubt and the tendency to minimize your greatness.

4. On top of the salt, pour in a 1-inch layer of sugar. This encourages you to speak to and think of yourself with kindness.

5. On a sheet of paper that can fit in the jar without folding, make a list of six lovable things about yourself. Stick the paper into the sugar so it stands up and can be read.

6. Sprinkle the rose petals and lemon-peel hearts around your list. These will help you feel love without needing outside validation.

7. Place the rose quartz in front of the list to encourage you to be as kind to yourself as you are to others.

8. Light your candle and place it behind the jar, so the light illuminates your list and the magical ingredients surrounding it. Read the list out loud to yourself three times. Extinguish the candle when you feel finished.

9. Keep your jar and candle someplace you'll see it every day. Relight the candle and focus on your self-love jar anytime you need to be reminded of how wonderful you are.

Sweet Dreams

This jar is filled with ingredients that symbolize deep sleep, pleasant and prophetic dreams, and quieting the mind. Lepidolite's lithium content makes it a perfect crystal to facilitate a feeling of calm before bed, and celestite combines with the power of poppies to open the mind to the dreamworld. Rose quartz, salt, herbs, and that ancient cobalt blue color work together to provide protection from nightmares. These ingredients can help bring peace to the entire household throughout the night. This spell is best performed in the bedroom during a new moon, when people tend to sleep the longest and deepest.

4-ounce cobalt blue glass jar with lid

Salt

Dried lavender, jasmine, and chamomile flowers*

Poppy seeds

Small rose quartz, lepidolite, selenite, and celestite crystals

Lighter or matches

Purple, blue, or black chime candle

Plate

1. Start by preparing your bedroom environment. Gather your materials, close the bedroom curtains, and make the bed. Make sure everything is ready so you can peacefully slip into bed after casting this spell.

2. Layer the ingredients in the jar. Start with the salt, followed by the dried flowers and poppy seeds, and finish with the crystals on top. Close the lid tightly.

3. Light your chime candle. Hold the candle in one hand while you hold the jar over the plate with the other hand. Carefully drip candle wax around the lid of the jar until the edges are sealed.

4. Hold the jar in your hand, gaze upon the contents, and say "I am safe and at peace in the dreamworld."

5. Place the jar under or next to your bed. Get into bed and drift off to sleep.

6. Anytime you feel anxious or restless, repeat this spell by focusing on the jar and speaking the incantation.

*To brew a calming cup of tea before bed, mix these flowers in equal parts and add a teaspoon to boiling water. Not a tea person? Put your mixture into a bath instead. You can even add lavender, jasmine, and chamomile essential oils for extra fragrance.

Spring Cleansing Potion

This potion uses fresh spring water and flowers to invoke the cleansing energy of the vernal equinox. Tulips—one of spring's first flowers—are a magical symbol of love, protection, and good luck in new endeavors. Their vibrant but simple design is a reminder that things need not be complicated to be beautiful. With this potion, you can harness the power of springtime during any season.

Lighter or matches

Rose incense

Clear glass jar
  with airtight lid

Spring water

Pinch sea salt

1 teaspoon lime juice

6 drops geranium
  essential oil

Moss agate

Tulip

1. Gather your materials and set up near a window where sunlight is coming in, even if it's not bright.

2. Light the rose incense. Focus on the spring scene outside, or, if there isn't one, close your eyes and imagine the perfect spring day. Breathe in the incense and imagine flowers blooming all around you.

3. Fill the jar ¾ full with spring water. Imagine the smell of rain.

4. Add the sea salt, lime juice, and geranium oil.

5. Drop the moss agate into the jar. This crystal connects the potion to the cycles of nature.

6. Hold the tulip in your hands and whisper what you want to cleanse away, or what you want to grow in the future. Place it in the jar and allow it to float in the water. Set the jar on your windowsill and leave it for one hour.

7. Remove the tulip and crystal from the water. Replace the lid and shake to blend your potion.

8. Add this cleansing potion to floor and window washes or add to a spray bottle to clear the air. You can also pour a small amount into a bath to cleanse your auric field. Store it in the refrigerator for up to 2 weeks.

Soak the Pain Away

Baths connect you to the emotional and intuitive element of water, and the physical and mental effects of soaking in a warm bath are their very own type of magic. This blend features the calming power of lavender, oils to soothe and heal the skin, and Epsom salt, which helps relax swollen and sore muscles.

½ cup sea salt

2 cups Epsom salt

¼ cup baking soda

32-ounce mason jar with lid

⅛ cup dried lavender

⅛ cup dried yarrow

2 tablespoons carrier oil (sweet almond, olive, or jojoba oil)

Lavender and bergamot essential oils (as desired)

Tumbled clear quartz crystal

Metal spoon

Cloth drawstring bag

1. Start by adding the sea salt, Epsom salt, and baking soda to the jar. Next, add the dried lavender and yarrow, and mix everything together.

2. Slowly drizzle the carrier oil over the salts while mixing. Make sure you are continuously mixing, so as not to create any pools of oil.

3. One drop at a time, add the essential oils. Adjust the amount to be the most pleasurable for you.

4. Place the clear quartz in the jar to spread its healing energy to the rest of the blend. Clear quartz is also known as "The Master Healer" and can assist in any healing endeavor. Allow your salts to dry for a few hours, then close the jar.

5. At bath time, use the metal spoon to scoop ¼ to ½ cup of your potion into the cloth bag, along with the clear quartz.

6. Let the water from the faucet run through the bag. After you finish filling the tub, the bag can partially submerge in the water.

7. Tell the quartz where you need pain relief and imagine a bright white light emanating from the bag, surrounding that place with healing energy. When your bath is finished, remove the quartz (before pulling the plug), dry it off, and add it back to the jar for future baths.

Witch, Heal Thyself

Medicinal **herbalism is separate from** *magical* **herbalism, but medicinal plants are used in witchcraft for healing. The mundane (meaning earthly, or nonspiritual) uses of plants can still tell us a little about their magical energy. This herbal blend features some of the most powerful healing herbs, with the appropriately named self-heal plant as the star of the show. This spell jar is best prepared on a Sunday, the day of solar healing energy.**

Green bottle or jar with airtight lid

Lighter or matches

Cedar incense

Dried self-heal, motherwort, witch hazel, echinacea, mint, bay leaves, lavender, and mugwort

Tumbled green obsidian

1. Start by cleansing the bottle or jar. Light the cedar incense and use the smoke to cleanse your container and any other tools you're using.

2. Add equal parts of each of the dried herbs, filling the jar to the top.

3. Inhale the aromas of the cedar and herbs, the scent of a lush forest or field. Tune into the healing energy of these ingredients. Hold the green obsidian in your hand. Tune into the obsidian's green healing energy. Imagine the obsidian glowing in your hand, spreading its healing light throughout your aura.

4. Place the stone inside your jar and visualize the light filling every leaf, twig, and stem.

5. Let this spell serve as a beacon of healing energy. As needed, open the container and use the herbs. You can add them to baths, candles, charm bags, and even other container spells focused on healing.

Embodiment Oil

Massage has been healing humans around the globe for thousands of years. The oldest depiction of massage dates back to 2330 BCE in Egypt, and the practice remains an important part of maintaining health through natural means. Massage promotes relaxation and, when done by a professional, can relieve pain and heal injuries. Spiritually, massage connects us to our bodies and grounds us in the present.

1 ounce (30 milliliters) sweet almond oil

1-ounce (30-milliliter) amber glass bottle with cap

10 drops jasmine essential oil

5 drops lemongrass essential oil

10 drops patchouli essential oil

5 drops pink or black pepper essential oil

1 capsule (⅛ teaspoon) vitamin E oil

Small tumbled bloodstone

Marker

Adhesive label

1. Pour sweet almond oil into the amber bottle until it is almost full. Then add the remaining oils. Feel free to adjust the quantities to suit your tastes. Extra patchouli and pepper will be grounding, and additional lemongrass will clear the mind and bring in happy energy.

2. Hold the bloodstone and focus on its energies of physical healing, strength, and greater enjoyment of physical and sensual experiences.

3. Drop the stone into the bottle, then close the cap tightly. Gently shake it to mix all of the oils together with the energy of the bloodstone.

4. With the marker, write a simple affirmation on the label showing love or care for your body like "I appreciate everything my body does for me" or simply "I love my body." Affix the label to the jar.

5. To use, warm some oil between your hands and breathe deeply to inhale the magical aroma. Close your eyes and massage the oil into your skin, allowing it to draw your focus to your body.

Meditation Jar

Have you ever seen a lava lamp? The calm, slow movement of colorful bubbles and blobs of "lava" floating up and down is so relaxing. It clears your mind while keeping your focus. Inspired by glitter-filled lava lamps, this spell jar uses blue cornflower to help you settle into a meditative state and communicate with the universe.

Water

Empty tea bag

Blue cornflower

Lighter or matches

Frankincense

16-ounce (500-milliliter) glass jar or bottle with airtight lid

Metallic mica powder

Biodegradable glitter

Clear corn syrup

Dish soap

Blue and/or purple food coloring

Blue or violet chime candle and holder

Superglue (optional)

1. Bring ½ cup to 2 cups of water to a boil, then use the tea bag to steep 1 teaspoon of blue cornflower petals in the water. Allow the tea to cool until it is no longer hot, but still warm.

2. Light the frankincense and hold the jar in the path of the smoke. To cleanse away lingering energy, make sure the smoke touches the inside and outside of the jar.

3. Pour a layer of mica and glitter into the bottom of the jar. Make sure the layer is at least 1 inch thick.

4. Fill the jar ¼ full with clear corn syrup, then add three drops of dish soap.

5. Remove the bag of cornflower petals from the warm tea.

6. Add drops of blue and/or purple food coloring to the tea. When the color is to your liking, pour the tea into your spell jar, leaving about one inch of space at the top of the jar.

7. Light the candle and hold it over the jar so wax drips into it, forming little wax beads. You don't need many. When you're done, place the candle in the holder.

8. Cap your container tightly. If you're worried about spilling, superglue the edges of the lid. Shake the jar so everything gets mixed together.

9. To initiate meditation, place the candle behind the jar so the light shines through. Hold the spell jar horizontally and slowly rock it back and forth, breathing in time with the rhythm. You can also shake it like a snow globe, set it down, and meditate for as long as it takes for the glitter to settle at the bottom of the jar.

Nourishment Jar

Everyone loves tasty food, right? If only it were that simple. Fatphobia and rigid mainstream beauty standards can make it hard to craft a happy and empowering relationship with eating, no matter what size or shape you happen to be. This jar uses an optional image of Budai or Hotei, a semi-historical Chinese monk—commonly referred to as Laughing Buddha—who is worshipped in Chan Buddhism (Zen Buddhism in Japan). This is a very personal topic, so as you craft your jar, choose from the list of suggested ingredients based on what resonates most with you. Follow your gut, otherwise known as your intuition. Perform this spell during the full moon, a time of abundance and celebration.

Lighter or matches

Jasmine incense

Mason or hexagonal jar with lid

Glue

Drawing or printed image of Laughing Buddha

SUGGESTED STONES

Orange selenite—
separating the physical from the emotional needs of food

Peach moonstone—
healing for feelings of hopelessness regarding weight or body image

Rose aura quartz—
promoting self-worth, positive body image, and healing from fatphobic bullying

SUGGESTED TOOLS

Hemp rope—
binding together and accelerating magical time lines

Small mirror—
reflecting energy outward and ensuring mirrors show you a realistic and positive reflection

SUGGESTED BOTANICALS

Apple seeds—love and recognizing natural beauty

Bay leaves—strength and power

Cinnamon sticks—lust and sexual attraction

Coffee beans—waking up to the truth, changing mood and behavior

Hibiscus flowers—freedom and love

Jasmine—connecting the physical to the spiritual

Mint—clearing mental blocks and energizing the body

Motherwort—healing and nurturing

Rice—nourishing and fulfilling

Rose petals or buds—love, romance, and the ability to see the beauty within

Sugar—sweetening and joy

Sunflower seeds—nourishment and vitality

Tasty treats like nuts, dried fruit, candy—enjoying pure pleasure

1. Light the jasmine incense to connect your physical and spiritual selves. Jasmine also invokes the energy of sensuality.

2. As you add your ingredients into your jar, whisper what you want from each one.

3. If any of your chosen ingredients has a high moisture content, add a few grains of rice to absorb excess moisture.

4. Use glue to attach a depiction of the Laughing Buddha, often associated with happiness, good fortune, and a well-nourished body. Alternatively, use any depiction of nourishment and pleasure from food.

5. Place the jar on the kitchen counter where you can always see it, or tuck it into a cupboard with a mirror behind it, helping to reflect the energy outward.

CHAPTER FIVE

Spells for Abundance and Prosperity

• • • • • • • • • • • • • •

Ahh, money. We love it, we hate it, and we definitely need it. This is the second most popular branch of magic (love comes first) because it's universal and always necessary. The spells in this chapter will not only help you get money, but also help you see prosperity and abundance as something more than a number on a paycheck. Generosity, gratitude, pleasure, leadership, and recognition for your hard work all fall under this umbrella, and these spells make it rain.

Green Money Rice

Rice holds the power of abundance and prosperity in every grain. Green money rice is a traditional Hoodoo spell ingredient that can be used to attract prosperity and good luck, and this blend has never let me down.

3 cups white rice

Large glass bowl

Small bowl

1 tablespoon water

1 tablespoon Florida Water (see page 144) or good-quality alcohol

Green food coloring

Gold mica powder

Scissors

Paper money

Metal coins

Clear or green glass jar

1. Pour the rice into a large glass bowl. In a smaller bowl, mix the water and Florida Water with green food coloring. Add as little or as much color as you like. Slowly stir this liquid mixture into the rice.

2. Sprinkle gold mica powder over the rice, then allow it to dry for at least an hour.

3. Cut or shred a unit of paper money over the bowl, letting the pieces fall in. This makes the rice draw in that currency specifically. It also serves as a sacrifice or proof of dedication.

4. Mix in your metal coins, then transfer the rice mixture to the jar.

5. Let this spell jar serve as a beacon for prosperity and wealth or use the rice itself as an ingredient in future spells. Sprinkle the rice from the jar into your cash register or around your office to draw in business income, or into your wallet to fill your pockets.

Prosperity in Your Purse

Where do you keep your money? This tiny prosperity bottle can go with you anywhere. Whether you keep your money in a bank, purse, wallet, or safe, you can use this spell as a talisman for attracting new wealth and protecting your money. Craft this spell on a Thursday under the waxing moon, which promotes growth.

Green aventurine chips

Small bottle with cork top

Basil

Bay leaves

Gold leaf or glitter

Peppermint

Hot glue gun

Green, gold, or yellow chime candle

Lighter or matches

1. Start by placing half of the aventurine chips into the bottle. Layer the rest of the ingredients in any order. Then add another layer of aventurine on top, until the bottle is full. Aventurine's protective qualities safeguard the ingredients in the middle of the jar.

2. Use hot glue to affix the cork into the cap of the bottle.

3. Hold your candle and imagine yourself in a positive financial situation. This can be anything from winning the lottery to getting a raise at work.

4. Light the candle and hold it sideways so the wax drips over the top of the bottle and down the sides. This will seal in your intention.

5. Keep the bottle in your purse, pocket, car, or cash register.

Not-So-Piggy Bank

When used as a symbol of money, pigs can symbolize the selfish practice of hoarding more than your fair share. As cute as they are, let's replace the traditional piggy bank with a magical savings jar. Use this spell to home in on positive money symbols and intentions.

Lighter or matches

Cedar incense

Large green glass jar with lid

Green paint and brush (optional)

Four of Pentacles tarot card or printout

Chrysocolla—makes your dreams a reality

Emerald—makes money grow

Pyrite—luck

4 lucky coins

Sticky label and green or gold marker (optional)

Money or pay stubs

1. Light the cedar incense and cleanse your jar and materials in the smoke.

2. If your jar is clear, use green paint to cover it so you can't see what's inside. This will remove temptation to spend.

3. Ask the figure on the Four of Pentacles tarot card to hold fast to your money and keep it safe from theft or loss. Place the card in the jar.

4. Add your crystals to the jar, taking a moment to focus on the energy of each one. Chrysocolla makes dreams become reality, emerald brings financial growth, and pyrite brings luck.

5. Add your lucky coins to the jar, focusing on the energy of each coin. Consider using "magic money" like rare or antique coins.

6. If you're saving for something specific, write it on a label and attach it to the outside of the jar. This will keep you focused on your goal.

7. Every payday, add cash to the jar. If you don't have cash, add your pay stubs or a printed statement from your savings account.

Get-Noticed Oil

Oil of Abramelin is an ancient recipe with origins attributed to Jewish people living in Ancient Egypt. Made from olive oil and sacred botanicals, this oil was used to anoint the body before a ritual. A version of this ancient recipe was made popular by Aleister Crowley during the occult revival of the early twentieth century, though with slightly different ingredients and uses. Abramelin Oil also found its way into Hoodoo practices, within which cinnamon and calamus are used to attract good fortune. My version pays homage to all of these, with emphasis on the abundance and magic of the earth itself.

2 teaspoons extra-virgin olive oil, plus more as needed

Glass measuring cup

3 drops cinnamon essential oil*

7 drops myrrh essential oil

7 drops patchouli essential oil

1 capsule (⅛ teaspoon) vitamin E oil

Metal spoon

Small funnel

15- or 20-milliliter amber or orange glass bottle with cap (optional: with roller ball)**

Cannabis/hemp seeds***

Dried whole calamus root

1. Start by adding about 2 teaspoons of olive oil to the measuring cup.

2. Slowly add the essential oils and vitamin E to the measuring cup, then mix them together with a metal spoon. Add more fragrance if necessary.

3. Using the funnel, pour the oil blend into the bottle. Drop three cannabis seeds and three pieces of calamus root into the bottle as well. Top it off with olive oil and pour until the bottle is full. Replace the cap and shake. To use this spell as a perfume, apply a small amount of oil to your pressure points and solar plexus. Apply the perfume before you go into an interview or speak in front of a crowd. You can also add it to a spray bottle with water and a small amount-

Get-Noticed Oil of alcohol, then spray it around you. CONTINUED→

4. This oil can also be used an ingredient in other spells. If you're hoping to be chosen for a job or promotion, use the oil to dress an orange candle. Burn the candle on top of a honey jar (see page 93) that contains a business card or other career and prosperity materials.

*Cinnamon oil can cause skin irritation, so do a patch test before wearing.

**Note that orange glass does not diffuse sunlight the way amber does, which may lead to deterioration of ingredients within the bottle. Aside from that concern, orange glass and amber can be used interchangeably here.

***Always follow your local laws concerning cannabis.

Abundance vs. Prosperity

The words abundance and prosperity are often used interchangeably, but they do have different meanings. Prosperity refers to money or success in your career, and abundance refers to the gifts and blessings you have in life and how you share them. Regardless of how much money you have, you can be abundant in food, friends, positive experiences, or generosity. This spell will help you focus on the things in life that money can't buy and help you live an abundant life.

Magnetic or olivine sand

Mason jar

Empress tarot card or printout

9 small metal coins

Scissors

Brown paper

Green pen or marker

Emerald*

Citrine

Thin cloth and the ring from a mason jar lid

1. Pour a 1-inch layer of sand into the bottom of the jar and use it to prop up your tarot card. The Empress symbolizes abundance, financial independence, and a warm heart. Surround the card with your nine coins.

2. Focus on the card and think about abundance. How do you define it? How does abundance feel? How will you know if you've achieved it?

3. Cut out nine squares of brown paper. With your green pen, write a characteristic of abundance on each one. Fold them into smaller squares and put them in the jar.

4. Emerald is the ultimate stone of abundance, and citrine focuses on the joy you get from abundance and generosity. Hold the emerald to your heart and the citrine to your solar plexus. Imagine a mixture of green and yellow light surrounding you—emanating not from the crystals but from you. Fill the crystals with this light and say, "I am grateful for everything I have and for the opportunity to show generosity to others." Then place the emerald and citrine in the jar.

CONTINUED →

5. This jar should stay open. Keep the contents safe by removing the snap lid and using the ring to affix cloth over the jar's opening.

6. Keep the jar in the kitchen—your home's abundant heart—where you can see it.

*Emerald can be found in a raw form at crystal shops. You do not need the crown jewels.

Dissolving Financial Fears

No matter how much money we have, everyone develops certain behaviors and beliefs that may hold us back from reaching our goals. This spell helps dissolve these unproductive fears and beliefs so you can craft a healthier relationship with money. Perform this spell on Saturday after the full moon, during the waning phase.

Paper and pen	Dried lemongrass	Salt
Clear mason jar with airtight lid	Dried lavender	Vinegar
	Frankincense tears	Water
Metal coin		

1. Close your eyes, take a few deep breaths, and call up every worry or fear you have about your financial situation.

2. Write the money beliefs you hold about yourself specifically—things like "I'm bad with money" or "I don't deserve money."

3. Write all of your general beliefs about money, like "rich people are snobs" or "money is the root of all evil."

4. Fold the paper(s) together and place the square in the jar along with the coin.

5. Add a pinch each of lemongrass and lavender, which help transform fear and anxiety into more positive emotions. Add nine frankincense tears, making a promise to destroy these fears.

6. Pour a thick layer of salt over the ingredients and add vinegar until the jar is half full. Fill the rest with water, replace the lid, and shake the jar to mix it all together.

7. Keep the jar in a window and shake it once a day while you imagine all of these fears and anxieties inside you dissolving away.

8. On the night of the new moon, take your jar outside and dump it out.

Benevolent Boss Bell Jar

Being the boss is about a lot more than the paycheck and the glory; it's a position of service to others—your employees, your community, your company, yourself. Great power really does come with great responsibility, and this decorative display for your desk or office will help you fulfill these obligations, or help you develop these qualities for the future. This is a DIY spell with lots of suggested materials and instructions, so tap into your creativity and customize it to your needs.

Large decorative bell jar or clear mason jar

Visual representation of a leader

Tarot cards

Business cards

Writing utensils

Small glasses or bowls

SUGGESTED BOTANICALS

Allspice berries— determination and creativity

Cloves—quell gossip and misinformation

Coffee beans— eloquence and stamina

Get-Noticed Oil (page 55)

Green Money Rice (page 52)

Incense of sage, ginger, or frankincense

Master of the woods (sweet woodruff)— leadership and confidence

Nutmeg—loyalty and vision

Small succulent plants—job protection and workplace healing

SUGGESTED CRYSTALS AND STONES

Crystal pyramid— vision

Crystal sphere— widened influence

Crystal tower or obelisk—upward momentum

Jade—good fortune and longevity

Lapis lazuli— sovereignty and active listening

Pyrite—courage, focus, and defusing chaos

Rainbow opal—joy and satisfaction from work

Sunstone—confidence and creativity

1. Cleanse your workspace or work materials with incense for leadership, wisdom, or creativity. If incense is not welcome in your work area, try an essential oil diffuser or spray.

2. As you craft this spell in your jar of choice, use symbols associated with your job (or the job you want).

3. Focus on the qualities you want to embody as a boss or a coworker and choose ingredients accordingly. You can even write these qualities down on a business card for use in your display.

4. Experiment with different arrangements until it feels right.

5. Display the jar prominently on your desk or in your workspace.

SUGGESTED PRACTICES

- Include a tarot card featuring one of the kings or queens from the Minor Arcana or use an image of a leader you admire and wish to emulate.

- For upward momentum, place a crystal tower or obelisk on top of your business card. For vision, add a pyramid, and for influence, add a sphere.

- Place botanicals like berries and cloves into small bowls, or sprinkle them around the base of your jar.

- To help you get noticed for a new position, include the business card of the hiring manager. You can also create a mock business card or nameplate for your desired position and display it in the jar.

CHAPTER SIX

Spells for Inspiration and Motivation

• • • • • • • • • • • • • • • • • • •

Did you know that the brain chemical that makes you feel motivated is also responsible for making you feel happy and fulfilled? Passion and pleasure work together to help us reach important milestones, accomplish our goals, and share the very best of ourselves. The spells in this chapter work with unique ingredients and ideas to expand your mind, teach you something new about the universe, and help you craft fascinating creative works.

A Midsummer Night's Ink

Every summer the mulberry bushes in my city explode with fruit so juicy the sidewalks below are stained the color of the night sky. Mulberries are delicious (just ask the birds) and make for fantastic pies, but their fragility makes them difficult to sell commercially. That's why you won't find them at your local market. Their wild nature and relationship with winged animals make mulberries a combination earth and air element tool that can help you think outside the box and infuse your words with natural magic.

Saucepan

½ cup filtered water

1 tablespoon apple cider vinegar

2 cups ripe mulberries

Potato masher

Metal strainer

2 glass bowls

Cheesecloth or coffee filter

1½–2 teaspoons gum arabic (liquid or powder)

Funnel

Glass ink pot or small jar with airtight lid

3 drops clove essential oil

1. In a saucepan, bring the filtered water and vinegar to a boil, then add the berries. Let the mixture simmer for 20 to 30 minutes while you stir and mash with a potato masher.

2. Place the metal strainer over one glass bowl and pour the ink blend through it. Use a spoon to mash the berries. Once you've gotten as much juice as you can, discard the berries and rinse the strainer.

3. Place the strainer over a new glass bowl and line the inside of the strainer with cheesecloth or a coffee filter. Pour the ink through twice, replacing the filter or cloth each time.

4. In its current state, this potion can be used like watercolor paint. If you want a true ink you will need gum arabic. If using gum arabic in liquid form, add it directly to the ink. If using gum arabic in powder form, stir 2 teaspoons of powder into 4 teaspoons of hot water until it dissolves. Then add the gum arabic to the ink.

5. When the mixture has cooled down, pour it into your ink pot using the funnel. Add 3 drops of clove essential oil as a preservative and a magical deterrent to gossip and miscommunication.

6. Keep in the refrigerator and shake before using.

Chariot #7 Powder

This spell powder is filled with the energy of motivation. Inspired by the Chariot tarot card, this potent powder has a wide variety of uses. Employ its magic when you need a motivational boost in the physical, emotional, intellectual, or spiritual realm.

Lighter or matches

Cinnamon incense

Red bottle or jar with cap or lid

Mortar and pestle

Brown sugar

Cinnamon

Dried orange peel

Gold mica

Pepper

Dried chili flakes

Red clay

Rosemary

Salt

Bowl

Glue

Chariot tarot card or printout

1. Start by cleansing your container. Light the cinnamon incense and use the smoke to cleanse the bottle or jar inside and out.

2. Carefully waft the smoke from the incense around your feet, hands, and head. This will clear away anything that may be draining your energy and focus, including the desire to procrastinate, run away, or give up.

3. Use the mortar and pestle to grind any whole ingredients into powder. As you grind the powder, say any of the following incantations that applies to you.

"I am in the driver's seat on the road to my destiny."
"I take swift action and trust my instincts."
"I know my goals are attainable if I put in the time and energy."

4. Place equal parts of each blended ingredient into a bowl and mix them together.

5. Pour the mixture into the jar and use glue to affix your copy of the Chariot to the outside. This container is now bound to the magical creatures on the card, who will help you drive your chariot to victory.

SUGGESTED PRACTICES*

- To increase motivation for a specific goal, write the goal on a sheet of paper and set it on fire. Let it burn to ash, then mix the ashes with the Chariot #7 powder. Add the new mixture to a small bottle and carry it with you.

- To increase physical motivation, or to keep you from feeling "dead on your feet" for the day, sprinkle a small amount of powder into your shoes.

- To add a motivational energy to your spell work, use this powder to dress spell candles.

- To clear away distractions and boredom at work, sprinkle Chariot #7 powder at each of the four corners of your desk, then sweep the powder into the middle and toss it outside.

*Do not add this powder to baths, get it near eyes, or breathe it in.

Aura Inspiration Pendulum Bottle

A pendulum is a divination tool made from a heavy charm or crystal suspended on a chain. Pendulums are used as tools to focus energy and to divine messages from spiritual sources. This special pendulum bottle whips up an aura of inspiration to help you break through writer's block, come up with an innovative idea, or create your next masterpiece.

Lighter or matches

Frankincense incense

Drill or screwdriver

Pyramid-shaped clear glass bottle with cork or cap*

Aqua aura pendulum

Glue gun or dripping wax

White willow bark

Real gold leaf

Gold mica or glitter

1. Light the frankincense and use the smoke to cleanse yourself and your tools. This removes any energy that may block the spirit of inspiration from finding you.

2. Use a screwdriver or drill to make a hole in the middle of the cork or cap. String your pendulum through the hole so that the aqua aura hangs within the bottle. Make sure the crystal hangs low enough to swing, but not so low that it touches the bottom of the bottle or ingredients. Use hot glue or wax to keep the chain from falling through the hole and set it aside to dry.

3. In your bottle, sprinkle a thin layer of white willow bark. This lunar tree clears mental blocks and opens your mind for inspiration.

4. Sprinkle gold leaf into the bottle or add a piece of real gold jewelry. You can add more golden energy with mica powder or glitter. Gold is the metal of inspiration and creativity.

5. Hold the pendulum over the incense smoke and focus your energy on it until it starts to spin.

6. Lift the pendulum over your head and close your eyes. As it spins, imagine a cone of electric blue light starting to form around you. As it encases you, imagine your chakras opening and spinning in time with the light.

   - The crown chakra opens you to inspiration from the universe; the third eye brings inspiration from deep in your imagination.
   - The throat chakra inspires you with words and music.
   - In the heart, you're inspired by the energy of love.
   - The solar plexus glows with inspiration from positive and joyful experiences.
   - The sacrum allows you to draw inspiration from the world through both your physical and psychic senses.
   - Finally, the root chakra allows you to draw inspiration from nature and the planet.

7. When you feel the light flowing both in and out of all seven chakras, carefully replace the cap of the bottle. Swirl it in the same direction your pendulum was swinging before. That cone of light is contained inside the bottle, and anytime you need to draw power from it, simply give your bottle a swirl and imagine that light shining on everything you create.

*Having trouble finding a specialty shape? A large, round mason jar will also work. This spell needs a jar with a base that is wide enough to allow the pendulum to swing.

Neptune Planet Power

Neptune is the planet of dreams and imagination. It's helpful to invoke the power of Neptune when the real world is taking center stage in your mind and you're having trouble connecting to the things that make life magical. This spell will help inspire your next great work of art, provide psychic insights, and make your dreams a reality. Craft this spell on the night of the full moon.

Jasmine essential oil and diffuser	A potion bottle with cap	Pearls and/or seashells
Music	Cannabis seeds*	Sand
Sea glass	Larimar and/or aquamarine crystals	Sea salt
		Light blue candle

1. Diffuse jasmine essential oil in water so the aroma fills the room.

2. Put on music that feels dreamy and emotional, or that features oceanic sounds like waves or whales.

3. Set aside a piece of sea glass or a crystal. Layer the rest of the ingredients in the bottle in whatever order and quantity you feel called to.

4. Cap the bottle. Light the candle and drip candle wax over the top and around the edges of the cap it to seal the bottle. Before the wax cools, press the reserved crystal or glass into it.

5. Hold the bottle to your third eye and imagine a bright blue light emanating from it, spilling over you like a wave. Channel the energy into doing something artistic, like dancing or singing along to the music.

6. Keep the bottle next to your bed at night to charge it with the magic of your dreams. This will allow new ideas and images to come to you.

*Always follow your local laws concerning cannabis.

Uranus Planet Power

Uranus is the planet of freedom, curiosity, and "shaking things up." It's a planet that loves revolutionary change, innovative ideas, eccentricity, and genius. The atomic element uranium, named for this giant of the sky, shares its association with big brains and big change. You can harness the energies of both the element and the planet to help you make groundbreaking discoveries. This spell will help you reach creative and intellectual enlightenment.

Uranium glass container (optional: with lid)*

Dirt from your yard

Dirt from a school, library, or other place of learning

Ground coffee

Ground cloves

Witch hazel

Brown paper and blue pen

Lapis lazuli stone

5 small fluorite crystals or chips

Black light or UV light (optional)

1. Fill the container ⅔ full with equal parts dirt from your home and a place of learning. Add a pinch of coffee for motivation, cloves to help you believe in yourself, and witch hazel to remind you that every discovery has the potential for good and bad. This spell will inspire you to focus on the good.

2. Tear off five strips of brown paper. On each strip, use a blue pen to write your goals or intentions for this spell, like "my experiments yield fascinating results" or "my work changes people's lives for the better." Or describe any projects you're working on that have Uranian potential. Fold up each paper and press it into the dirt in your container.

3. Next, bury the lapis lazuli in the center of the dirt, drawing on its ability to expand mental capacity and open the mind to magical knowledge.

4. On the table or surface around the jar, arrange the fluorite crystals in a pentagon shape. These will keep you grounded while allowing your mind to travel beyond the limits of convention.

CONTINUED➔

5. If you have one, now is the time to turn on your UV or black light and take in the fluorescent glow.

6. Pick up the container with both hands, using one to cover the opening or keep the lid in place. While giving the container a shake, speak one of the goals or ideas you wrote down earlier. Repeat this process for all five, then place the jar back in the center of the fluorite pentagon.

7. Keep this jar assembled for the duration of your project. Anytime you feel you've hit a dead end or need to see things from a new angle, fire up your black light and shake things up.

> *Uranium glass is a specialty collectible item, but this spell can be done with another jar of your choosing. Special materials like this can add a little something extra to your spells, but never limit yourself because you don't have something rare or expensive. Many of the more common materials in this spell are already associated with the planet Uranus. Select a container that is unique and paint it with UV or glow-in-the-dark paint to get the fluorescent experience.

Confidence Charm

This tiny bottle charm can be worn around your neck to help you call up your inner reserves of confidence. This spell is an excellent way to tune into your own emotional strength and draw on the passionate energy of the sun.

Lighter or matches

Gold or yellow chime candle in holder

2 bay leaves, divided

Sheet of aluminum foil

1.5-milliliter miniature glass bottle with cork

Calendula petals

Sunflower seed

Small citrine crystal

Small tiger eye crystal

Miniature gold screw-in eyelet pin

Yellow string or gold necklace chain

1. Light the candle and focus on the flame. Feel the warmth radiating from it.

2. Using the flame of the candle, light a bay leaf and carefully use the smoke to cleanse the bottle, ingredients, and yourself. Place the leaf on the foil to finish burning as incense.

3. Open your bottle and add a pinch of calendula petals to move stagnant energy.

4. Next, add a sunflower seed to radiate strength and a small bay leaf for victory.

5. Finally, add citrine for good luck and tiger eye for creativity and confidence.

6. Replace the cork tightly and screw the eyelet pin into the middle of it.

7. Carefully lift your candle and drip wax over the cork to seal in your ingredients and bind them with the energy of fire.

8. String the bottle on a yellow string or gold chain and wear around your neck for confidence.

Tea to Clear Brain Fog

This tea blend is based on the London Fog, a latte made with sweetened Earl Grey tea, vanilla, and botanicals. Ironically, the ingredients in most versions of the drink possess the magical energy to clear out brain fog.

Tumbled clear quartz crystal

8-ounce clear jar with lid

Salt

Water

1 cup Earl Grey tea

½ cup blue cornflower petals

¼ cup lavender buds

1 vanilla bean, chopped

Tea bag or infuser

Teacup

Sugar or honey

½ cup steamed milk (optional)

1. Start by cleansing the energy of your jar and quartz. Place the quartz in the jar with a pinch of salt. Add an inch of water. Swirl the salt water in a counterclockwise motion three times. Rinse out and dry the jar, removing and drying the quartz as well.

2. Add the tea, cornflower petals, lavender buds, and vanilla to the jar. Take a moment to focus on the properties of each one.

   Earl Grey—Black tea energizes the mind and magically enhances memory, and bergamot helps you notice and focus on important details.
   Blue cornflower—opens the third eye and clears out intuitive blocks
   Lavender—calms the mind and offers spiritual protection
   Vanilla—restores lost mental and spiritual energy

3. Hold the quartz up to your third eye and say, "I can see through my mind's eye with magical clarity." Place the crystal in the jar.

4. Cap the jar and gently shake it to blend the tea with the energy of the quartz.

5. **To brew the tea:** Bring 8 ounces of water to a boil. Add a heaping teaspoon of Tea to Clear Brain Fog to a tea bag or infuser. Place the quartz from the jar into the hot water, and steep with the tea bag for no more than 3 to 5 minues. Stir counterclockwise and sweeten with sugar to taste. Drink as is or make a latte by mixing with ½ cup of steamed milk. As you drink your tea, repeat the incantation from step 3. Feel your mind's eye open to new possibilities and perspectives. Let any fog or confusion drain away with every sip.

6. When finished, wash and dry the quartz and return it to the jar for future use.

Court of Wands Oil

The court cards in the tarot Suit of Wands are intelligent and authoritative figures capable of immense creativity. Their fiery nature makes them symbols of artistry, adventure, creation, spirituality, and power. Create an oil blend inspired by your favorite member of the Court of Wands using any of the suggestions here. For a large burst of creative energy, craft this spell during the full moon phase. To grow a creative skill or idea over time, craft this spell during the waxing phase of the moon.

Tarot court card from the Suit of Wands (king, queen, knight, or page)

Funnel

15-milliliter amber bottle with roller ball

Sweet almond oil

9 to 17 drops essential oils (see list that follows)

1 capsule (⅛ teaspoon) vitamin E oil

SUGGESTED ESSENTIAL OILS

Allspice—courage

Basil—beauty and luck

Cannabis—innovative ideas*

Cardamom—romance and sexuality

Cinnamon—creativity

Citronella/ lemongrass—mental clarity

Coffee—increased energy and drive

Dragon's Blood—imagination and fantasy

Ginger—passion

Lotus—spiritual guidance

Mint—eloquence

Palo santo—spiritual protection

Patchouli—working with your body, sensuality

Rosemary—remembrance and connection to history

Sandalwood—intuition and magic

Sweet orange—interest and enthusiasm

1. Place your chosen tarot card nearby. Use the funnel to fill the bottle with sweet almond oil, leaving a little room at the top.

2. Choose your essential oils based on their scent and magical energy. Close your eyes and breathe in the aroma before slowly adding each one to the bottle. Does the scent conjure to mind any of the motifs on your court card?

3. Let your bottle sit open for 10 minutes. Walk away to clear your nose, then return to smell your creation.

4. Top the bottle off with vitamin E oil and sweet almond oil.

SUGGESTED PRACTICES

- Use the oil to anoint your pulse points, third eye, solar plexus, art supplies, musical instruments, and spell candles.

- Diffuse the oil in a room where you're working on creative projects.

- Wear as a perfume while exhibiting your creative skills or projects.

- Smell the oil to clear creative blocks and inspire ideas.

- Anoint your court card with a drop of oil and carry it as a magical talisman.

*Always follow your local laws concerning cannabis.

CHAPTER SEVEN

Spells for Boundaries and Protection

• • • • • • • • • • • • • • • • •

lack cats, evil eyes, twisted truths, and fortified thresholds: Spells for boundaries and protection are the root of all container magic. The use of bottles and jars is most prevalent with this branch of magic. These spells can be cast for protection from other people, natural disasters, psychic intrusion, and even ourselves. Although these spell jars cannot guarantee that nothing bad will ever befall you, they can empower you to fight against adversity. Use these spells to lay claim to your own personal powers of protection and healing.

Classic Witch Bottle

The original purpose of a witch bottle was to protect the home from evil and illness perpetrated by man or magic. Like African bottle trees, this jar serves as a trap for evil spirits and energy. Malicious energies get stuck on the sharp objects and become neutralized by the salt.

Lighter or matches

Rosemary incense

Mason jar or bottle with airtight lid

Salt

Nails

Pins

Needles

Thorns

Dirt from your property

Red wine or red wine vinegar

Black candle

1. Light the rosemary incense and use the smoke to cleanse the inside and outside of your container. Walk around your home wafting smoke around every door and window to clear away any vulnerabilities or negative energy.

2. Add salt to the jar, then alternate layers of sharp items and salt until the container is nearly full. Add a handful of dirt from your property to tie the magic to your home.

3. Measure out 1 ounce (a shot glass) of red wine. Take a sip and pour the rest into the spell. Red wine vinegar can be used if you don't imbibe, though I don't recommend taking a sip of it.

4. Replace the lid, light the black candle, and drip the wax over the lid to seal the spell.

5. Tuck the witch bottle out of sight somewhere near the main entrance or a kitchen cabinet. If you're doing renovations, you can also place it inside a wall or under a loose floorboard just like a classic European witch bottle.

Malocchio Magic Bottle

The evil eye (or *il malocchio* in Italian) is a catchall curse popular in Mediterranean countries. Someone can inadvertently cast this curse when they are feeling jealousy or sticking their nose where it doesn't belong. To protect from this curse, cobalt blue glass is fashioned into charms featuring an evil eye (*nazar* in Turkish). This charm can be hung in windows and on doors to prevent this curse from entering the home. It can also be worn as jewelry for personal protection. This bottle blends the magic of the evil eye with the most ancient spell of protection. When any negative energy is thrown your way, this spell works to convert it into something positive and grant you the privacy you need.

Paper and pen

Red string

Salt

Rue

Rosemary

Dried chili flakes

Cobalt blue bottle or jar with cap

Eye charm*

1. On a small strip of paper, write the following prayer:

   Evil eyes and jealous words
   are neutralized with salt and herbs.
   I am safe in all that I do
   as long as the sun comes shining through.

2. Roll up the paper and tie a red string around it.

3. Place a pinch each of salt, rue, rosemary, and dried chili flakes into the bottle. Add your spell scroll to the bottle as well and replace the cap.

4. Wrap a red string around the bottleneck nine times and attach the eye charm. Leave enough string to hang the bottle in a window where the sunlight can shine through.

*If you don't have a charm in the shape of an eye, paint one on the bottle with light blue and white paint, like the *nazar*.

Forged in Fire

Change is scary, but it's necessary for creation and growth. A volcanic eruption is not without tragedy, but without this fiery force of nature we wouldn't have islands such as Hawaii or magic crystals such as obsidian. We wouldn't see new islands rising out of the ocean, waiting to be discovered and explored. If you avoid or run from powerful transformation out of fear (it happens to the best of us), this volcanic spell can help you remain stable as you ride out the waves of change.

Volcanic sand or rocks

Pyramid-shaped bottle with metal cap*

Sea salt

Blue beryl crystal

Obsidian crystal

Lighter or matches

2 orange chime candles

Journal (optional)

1. Start by adding volcanic sand or rocks to your bottle. The sand represents the earth, solid but not still.

2. Next, add the salt followed by the crystals. The blue beryl represents the tumultuous ocean waves that breed new life. Obsidian symbolizes the beautiful results of riding out the waves of change.

3. Replace the cap on the bottle. Use a flame to heat the bottom of one of the orange chime candles. Affix the candle to the top of the bottle.

4. For the hour that the candle burns, take time to ground your energy. Think about your future like the beautiful obsidian gifts waiting for you when the eruption dies down. Allow the soft glow of the candle to calm you down, burn away your fears, and empower you to take the next steps with your head held high.

5. Repeat this ritual anytime big changes threaten to overwhelm you, or you lose sight of your goals.

6. If you find journaling empowering, use your volcano bottle like a timer and spend the hour writing out your fears as well as your dreams about the future. List the steps you need to take to achieve your goals and the skills and experience you already have to help you along the way.

*The pyramid shape will most resemble a volcano, but you can also use a bottle of any shape for that tapered look. A container in the shape of a stable square or fluid circle would also work wonderfully.

Truth to Power Oil

When it comes to setting boundaries, many of us feel it's rude to assert ourselves or ask the people around us for concessions—but this is actually an act of strength and respect. The essential oils in this blend are associated with speaking the truth, being understood, and having the courage to assert your boundaries with both enemies and friends. Craft this oil during the new moon. Take note that this spell works best if it can sit overnight and be collected earlier in the morning.

Small black onyx stone

15-milliliter blue or ultraviolet bottle with roller ball

2 drops black pepper essential oil

3 drops cedarwood essential oil

3 drops clove essential oil

3 drops juniper essential oil

Sweet almond oil

1 capsule (⅛ teaspoon) vitamin E oil

2 drops geranium essential oil (optional)

Square adhesive label and black pen

1. Place the onyx, a stone of protection and willpower, into the bottle.

2. Fill the rest of the bottle with the oils, taking a moment to breathe in the aroma of each one. If you want to assert boundaries in a romantic relationship specifically, add geranium oil to help you feel more comfortable expressing intimate emotions.

3. Replace the cap and shake well to blend the ingredients.

4. On a label that is square, symbolizing stability, draw the glyph for the planet Saturn, ♄, signifying boundaries. Surround the glyph with a circle to represent the new moon. Affix the label to the bottle.

5. Leave the bottle on the windowsill overnight. Collect it in the morning before the sunlight can hit it.

6. Apply the oil to your throat, heart, and palms whenever you need to speak with strength.

Motor City Magic

This spell jar induces a magical aura of protection and good fortune around your car and its occupants. A unique ingredient in this spell is Fordite or "Detroit agate." Though it looks like a colorful agate crystal, Fordite is made from automotive paint that dripped in layers over decades, hardened, and has been cut and polished like a crystal. Some date back to the 1940s. In magic, Fordite helps keep your car beautiful and running like a dream.

Salt

Dried comfrey leaf

Dried eyebright herb

Dried mugwort leaf

Small jar, large enough to fit a car key

Spare car key

Fordite

Moonstone

Snow quartz crystal

1. Add equal parts salt, comfrey, eyebright, and mugwort to the jar, filling it nearly to the top. Leave room for the crystals. Use your spare key to mix the ingredients together.

2. Take a moment to connect to the energy of each crystal.

   Fordite—keeps the car beautiful, invoking the magic of the Motor City
   Moonstone—protects over and around water
   Snow quartz—protects from harmful weather

3. Add your crystals on top of the salt and herb mixture.

4. Bring the spell jar to your vehicle. Open the car windows, turn on the radio, and find a song you love. (A Motown track, perhaps?)

5. Sprinkle a pinch of the salt and herb blend under each seat while you sing along to the song on the radio. Imagine a beautiful road stretching out before you as you ride in the car, with no fear or anxiety.

6. When the song is over, close the jar tightly and tuck it inside the glove box. Repeat before any long drives or when you're concerned about inclement weather.

Familiar Fortune

There are two kinds of people in this world—those who thrill at the sight of a black cat crossing their path, and those who feel their luck has suddenly run out. For many people, a black cat serves as a bad omen. For witches and other magical practitioners, black cats are trusted friends, symbols of resilience and cunning, and the living embodiment of good fortune. This spell honors and exudes the energy of the magical cat to offer spiritual protection and bless you with the ability to land on your feet, no matter how far you fall. It can also serve as a protection and good luck talisman *for* cats, as long it has a tight-fitting cap so it can be safely placed near their food or bed.

Lighter or matches

Mint incense

Black cat-shaped bottle with lid, or a container with the image of a black cat on the outside

3 pennies*

3 dimes

3 nickels

Clovers (4-leaf if possible)

Leopardskin jasper or cat's eye stone

Pinch catnip

Pinch silvervine

Pinch valerian root

Cat fur, nail trimmings, and whiskers**

1. Light the mint incense and use the smoke to cleanse the bottle, ingredients, and your hands.

2. Add the ingredients to the bottle one at a time, saving the fur, nails, and whiskers for last.

3. If the cat material is from one with which you share your home, invite them over to where you're working. Show them what you've collected and the spell you're crafting and thank them for their help. Share a pinch of the catnip, valerian, or silvervine with them to show your appreciation. If you don't live with the cat who contributed to your spell, send them a mental message of thanks and offer them some of the herbs the next time you see them.

4. Tightly seal the bottle with the lid and place it near the front door. Whenever you leave or return home, give your spell bottle a little pat to ask for good luck or protection, and thank it for doing a wonderful job.

*This spell uses American units of currency. Use coins that are most accessible to you based on your location.

**Never cut, pull out, or forcibly remove fur or whiskers from a cat. Use what falls naturally or pamper a cat with a brushing and a manicure to collect your ingredients.

Witch's Salt

Salt is the ultimate magical ingredient of protection and clearing away negative or harmful energy. Any kind of salt can serve this purpose, but this Witch's Salt uses deep earth magic to super-charge its protective power. The basic ingredients in this blend are salt from land and sea, charcoal, and ashes, but you can add any number of the ingredients listed to tailor-make a blend that works for you. I have included a list of magical herbs as well. Create this salt during the new moon and leave under the moonlight through the waxing phase to make the power grow.

Himalayan or table salt

Sea salt

Ultraviolet glass bottle or jar with cap

Mortar and pestle

Lighter or matches

Charcoal disk (for incense)

SUGGESTED POWDERS AND ASHES

Alfalfa—protect from drought and hunger

Angelica—call on guardian angels

Basil—protect from insecurities and low self-esteem

Black mustard seed (Eye of Newt)—protection for witches

Black pepper—banishing evil

Cedar—protect money or inheritance

Charcoal powder—invisibility and privacy

Clove—stop gossip and hateful words

Dragon's blood resin—fiery wall of protection, good fortune

Fennel—keep away police, IRS, nosy landlords

Garlic—drive away illness

Heather—healing and protection from domestic/sexual predators

Lemongrass/citronella—drive away insects and pests

Mugwort—psychic protection and safe travel

Mullein—neutralize a fear of the dark

Peony—safeguard against faeries and tricksters

Red brick dust—keeping out intruders

Rose—healing and protection from heartbreak

Rosemary—protect family members and beseeching ancestors

Rue—protect from the evil eye

Sage—banish spiritual entities

Vervain—bounce back magic cast against you

1. Add the salt varieties in equal parts to your jar.

2. If using pepper, mustard seed, brick dust, or incense resin, grind your selections with a mortar and pestle. Do not burn these ingredients for use as ashes.

3. If using ashes from herbs, burn the herb on a charcoal disk to produce ashes.

4. Add your desired ingredients to the jar and mix with the salt blend.

SUGGESTED PRACTICES

- To protect the home, pour a line of Witch's Salt across thresholds and windowsills.

- To prevent walking into danger, dust Witch's Salt onto the soles of shoes.

- To prevent nightmares, sprinkle under the bed.

- Cast a candle spell for protection by dressing black candles with oil and sprinkling them with Witch's Salt.

- Fill a small bottle with Witch's Salt, seal the lid with black wax, and carry it as a protection talisman.

CHAPTER EIGHT

Spells for Relationships and Romance

● ●

Is there any nobler magical goal than to give and receive love? Romance, friendship, sex, and breakups are some of the most significant, and emotional, human experiences. The heart chakra is not just the seat of our romantic feelings, but also of our inner peace. The love we have for ourselves and others comes from the same place as our love of life. That's why losing any love at all can be devastating. Magic can't make someone love you against their will, nor can it instantly remove the pain of heartbreak. But it can help you mend your wounds and find healthy ways to share love with the world around you.

Classic Honey Jar Petition Paper

Hoodoo is not a religion, but a set of practices created by enslaved Africans in the southern United States. It is inspired by many African traditional religions, Haitian vodou, Southern Baptist Christianity, and folk magic practiced by European colonizers and the local Indigenous people. Hoodoo is not closed to outside practitioners, but it's important for outsiders to be mindful and respectful of those who created any particular branch of magic.

One of the most popular Hoodoo spells is called a Honey Jar or Sweetening Spell. Crafting this magic technically involves two spells—the petition paper and the honey jar itself. Let's start with the petition paper, which binds the targets of the spell together and tells the magic exactly who needs sweetening.

Scissors	Small cup or bowl	One hair from each person
Paper	Red pen	

1. Cut a blank sheet of paper into a square, then use a small bowl or cup to trace a faint outline of a circle almost the same size as the paper itself.

2. In the middle of the paper, write the name of your love three times in red pen. Turn the paper 90 degrees to the right and write your own name three times, one on top of the other.

3. Using the circle as a guide, write your intention for the spell in a loop so it all connects. It could be a whole sentence, or "_____ loves _____" repeated as many times as possible. Here's the tricky part—you have to write the whole loop without lifting your pen from the page. Don't dot your i's or cross your t's. Don't worry about legibility.

4. Tie the hairs together if you can, then place them onto your petition paper. Fold the paper in half toward you with the hair tucked inside. Turn it 90 degrees to the right and fold it toward you again, and then one more time for a total of three. Each time, repeat your intention and the names of the lovers.

Classic Honey Jar for Sweet Romance

This is a traditional honey jar spell to attract a kind and loving romantic partner. It also helps you be a kind and loving partner in return. The idea of this spell is to draw someone in, making them see you in a positive and affectionate way. Sweetening spells can also be used to get a job, encourage a bully to stop bothering you, get a raise, or encourage someone to vote in your favor.

Hexagonal jar with metal lid

Honey

Classic Honey Jar Petition Paper (page 92)

2 rose petals

Small glass bowl

Metal teaspoon

1 teaspoon sweet almond oil

2 drops cinnamon essential oil

4 drops rose essential oil

Taper candle in red, pink, orange, or white

Lighter or matches

1. Fill the jar to the top with honey. Take a spoonful of honey from the jar and say, "As this honey is sweet to me, so, too, will I become sweet to _____." Repeat this process three times.

2. Push the Classic Honey Jar Petition Paper and two rose petals down into the honey, then close the jar.

3. In the small glass bowl, use the metal teaspoon to blend the sweet almond oil with the essential oils.

4. Choose a taper candle for your spell—red for passion, pink for romance, orange for attraction, or white, which can stand in for any color. While focusing on your goal, put a few drops of the oil blend on your hand and apply the oil to the candle in an upward motion.

5. Using a lighter, warm the wax on the bottom of the candle. As the wax begins to melt, affix it to stand on the lid of the honey jar. Light the candle and allow it to burn all the way down, letting the wax drip and embrace the sides of the jar.

6. Repeat this ritual by burning a new candle on top of the jar every Friday, the day ruled by Venus, for as long as it takes.

I Love Lamp

Romance, like witchcraft, is all about sending out the right vibe—setting the mood. In both cases, the soft glow of a flickering flame is the perfect way to start raising the energy you need. Like candles, oil lamps release a beautiful aroma and create a soft, warm glow. They can also be customized to match your magical purposes.

Alkanet root

8-ounce glass jar

Light olive oil*

One fresh rose

Tumbled rose quartz crystal

2 drops cardamom essential oil

4 drops rose essential oil

2 drops sandalwood essential oil

Stir stick

Floating wick

Lighter or matches

1. Sprinkle some alkanet root into the bottom of the jar, then fill the jar ½ full with olive oil. Let it sit for a few minutes, then give it a stir to release some of the color.

2. Remove the head of the rose from the stem and gently open the petals. Nestle the rose quartz into the flower and press it under the surface of the oil. Make sure your rose is totally submerged and sitting on the bottom of the jar.

3. Add more olive oil until it's an inch from the top of the jar. Add the essential oils and give them a quick stir.

4. When the time comes to set the mood, dab a little bit of the oil onto your neck like perfume, place a floating wick on top of the oil, and let there be light.

*Light olive oil is the only household oil I recommend, because it won't catch fire or produce smoke. I also recommend small floating wicks versus long ropes because they are less likely to result in a large flame. The glass will get hot, so oven mitts are recommended if you need to move it.

Chocolate-Covered Strawberry Salts

There is a mainstream belief that romance has to come from or exist for a significant other, or someone you're dating. This is a myth. Romance is just a creative expression of love. When performed alone, romance becomes a radical act of self-care. These bath salts will treat your body to a little luxury, your mind to a little euphoria, and your soul to the healing power of love. You can prepare this spell anytime, then use it for a bath on the night of a full moon.

Glass mixing bowl

2 tablespoons cocoa butter

2 tablespoons sweet almond oil

1 cup Epsom salt

1 cup Himalayan salt

1 teaspoon honey (optional)

1 tablespoon unsweetened cocoa powder

½ cup freeze-dried strawberry powder

6 drops strawberry fragrance oil

Tumbled strawberry quartz crystal

Heart-shaped bottle

Metal spoon

1. Using the glass bowl, melt the cocoa butter in the microwave in 30-second intervals. Then mix in the sweet almond oil.

2. Add the salts and honey to the bowl. When they are saturated, sprinkle in the cocoa powder and strawberry powder. Add the drops of strawberry fragrance oil. Mix well. Leave to dry overnight.

3. Hold the strawberry quartz crystal to your heart chakra and say six romantic things about yourself out loud. Strawberry quartz helps us break the cycle of self-doubt and become more aware of our self-worth. It combines the excited energy of romance with the grounding influence of honesty.

4. Transfer your salt mixture to the bottle and add the strawberry quartz.

5. On the night of a full moon, add the strawberry quartz and ½ cup of the salts to a warm bath. Feel free to put on romantic music or combine your bath with another pampering activity you enjoy. Allow yourself to enjoy this bath and the time you have to yourself.

Cutting Cords

When a relationship ends, you feel a loss in your life. It doesn't matter whether the relationship was good or bad. Suddenly, some part of our daily ritual is missing. To avoid this destabilizing possibility, we sometimes hold on to relationships that don't make us happy. Cord cutting is a ritual of letting go so both you and the other person can move on. Craft this spell when you need help getting through the end of a relationship, or when you need help summoning the courage to let go.

Lighter or matches

Dragon's blood incense

Aluminum foil

Paper and pen

Dried chili flakes

2 (4-ounce) glass or ceramic jars with lids

Dried lavender buds

Vinegar

Table salt

2 black chime or taper candles

String—red for romantic partner, pink for family, yellow for friends, white for work colleagues

Lighter or matches

1. Start by preparing your environment. Light dragon's blood incense and use the smoke to cleanse your tools and yourself. Cut a sheet of foil a foot long to cover your workspace.

2. Tear a sheet of paper in half down the middle. On the left side of the paper, write the full name and birthdate of the person you want distance from. Then write a short letter explaining why you want distance. Sign your name along with "I release you from this relationship with love."

3. Sprinkle dried chili flakes onto the paper and fold it into a small square packet. Place it in one of the jars.

4. On the other half of the ripped paper, write your name and birthdate. Then write yourself a letter about why you deserve this freedom, and what you will gain from enforcing this boundary. Focus on the future, not the past.

5. Sprinkle some dried lavender on this sheet and fold it just like you did the other packet, then place it in the other jar.

6. Pour a capful of vinegar over each packet, then fill each jar ¾ full with salt.

7. Stick a black candle into the salt of each jar. Place each jar on the foil.

8. Tie a 9-inch length of string into a circle and twist it twice in the middle so it looks like the infinity symbol. Align the knot with the twisted middle of the symbol to prevent it from catching fire.

9. Wrap each loop around a candle and pull the jars apart so the string stays looped around the top half of the candles without sliding down.

10. Light the candles. When the flame reaches the cord, it will catch fire and break, releasing you from each other for good. The foil should catch the burnt string and embers, but stay nearby with something to tamper the flame just in case.*

11. Let both candles burn down, seal the jars, and dispose of them in two different garbage cans.

*Witches work with fire a lot. Always be sure you have a working fire extinguisher and that you know how to contact the fire department.

Dream a Little Dream of Me

After a fight or separation, it can be hard to express your apologies or regrets. It can be even harder to accept an apology from someone who hurt you. This spell bottle helps you send a message of forgiveness or repentance through the world of dreams—a place where everyone is open to things they never thought possible. This spell is best performed around the full moon, when psychic and prophetic dreams are more vivid.

Light blue glass bottle with stopper

Salt water

Parchment-style paper and pen

Twine

Amethyst

Jasmine buds

Lavender buds

Cornflower petals

3 light blue chime candles

Sweet pea essential oil

Lighter or matches

Oil diffuser (optional)

Dream journal (optional)

1. Cleanse the bottle inside and out with salt water and leave it to dry in moonlight.

2. On the sheet of paper, write the name and birthdate of the person you're trying to contact. In a few short sentences, detail what went wrong.

3. Next, write a letter telling them your feelings and that you want to reconcile. End the letter with "If reconciliation is a dream we share, reach out to me and mend this tear." Then write your name and birthdate.

4. Roll the letter up and wrap twine around it three times, before tying it in a knot or bow. Slip it into the bottle.

5. Add as many amethyst chips, jasmine buds, lavender buds, and cornflower petals as you like. Take a moment to reflect on the purpose of each one. Amethyst conjures the power of dreams, and jasmine promotes psychic dreaming. Lavender symbolizes inner peace and healing, along with cornflower's powers of reconciliation.

6. Cap the bottle. Dress one of the blue chime candles with sweet pea oil to tune in to truth and emotional strength. Light the candle and hold it over the bottle. Let the wax drip and seal the cap.

7. Repeat this ritual for three nights, focusing on the letter you wrote and person you want to reach.

8. Keep the dream bottle next to your bed while you sleep and diffuse some of the sweet pea oil in your room to keep yourself focused.

9. If you keep a dream journal, rest the bottle on top of your journal while you sleep. Every morning, write down what you dreamed of— are there any messages related to this relationship?

10. After three days, reach out to your friend. If it doesn't work, put the bottle away until the full moon approaches again and repeat the process.

Best Witches Forever

My favorite kind of friendship bracelet features a charm of a heart in two pieces, with each friend getting one half of the heart. The charm symbolizes holding a special place in the heart of the other person, and a willingness to give up a piece of your own heart for them. These friendship charm bottles are inspired by that beautiful bit of childhood magic. You can make these bottles on your own and present them as a gift or make them with your friend.

Paper and pen

String (choose your favorite colors)

2 small bottles with cork stoppers

Rose quartz crystal chips

2 birthstones for each person

Small yellow rose or yellow rose petals

Dried orris (iris) root

Cloves

Magnolia

Friendship charms

1. On a small strip of paper, write down the qualities that make this person such a special and valuable friend. On another strip, write out all the things you pledge to do to be a good friend in return.

2. Roll up each strip and tie them with string. Then drop one scroll in each bottle, noting which is which.

3. Place a rose quartz chip and a birthstone for each person in both bottles.

4. Add the yellow rose, orris root, cloves, and magnolia, focusing on the meaning of each as you drop them in. Rose quartz and yellow roses symbolize friendship, and orris root signifies unconditional love. Cloves stop gossip, and magnolia represents loyalty without a loss of self.

5. Repeat your friendship pledge. Replace the corks.

6. Tie the string around the neck of each bottle and attach the charms.

7. Give the bottle with your friendship pledge to your friend. If you ever forget why your relationship means so much to you, open the bottle and read the list of things you love about them.

Unhurt My Heart

The heart chakra isn't just the seat of romantic love. The heart chakra is the home of all the love we carry with us. A healthy heart chakra is brimming with compassion, empathy, forgiveness, and trust. The Hindu name for this chakra, *anahata*, means "unhurt." With a healthy heart chakra, we can heal ourselves and others from the hurtful experiences we've been carrying within our hearts. This spell is inspired by the Japanese art of *kintsugi* or "golden repair." This method uses gold to fix broken objects, giving them new life and highlighting the beauty in flaws and scars. Choose from the suggested materials to personalize your heart-healing spell.

Heart-shaped glass bottle

Thick canvas bag

Hammer

Gloves

Clear epoxy adhesive

Powdered gold or gold mica

Wooden craft sticks

SUGGESTED ADDITIONAL MATERIALS

Heart-shaped charms

Love notes

Pressed flowers

Wedding or engagement rings

SUGGESTED CRYSTALS

Clear quartz—clearing away pain and fear

Morganite—unconditional love

Pink salt—emotional protection and clearing out negative energy

Raw emerald—harmony in the heart and in relationships

Rose quartz—heart healing

Ruby Fuchsite—opening the heart for self-reflection

Strawberry quartz—healing fears from past experiences

SUGGESTED BOTANICALS

Cocoa powder—grounding and a healthy heart

Dried apples and/or apple seeds—love divination, growth, and protection

Heather—healing from sexual or domestic abuse

CONTINUED →

Honeysuckle— sexuality and voluptuousness

Jasmine—sensuality and spiritual connection

Lavender—calming and healing

Peach, cherry, or plum stones— growing sensuality

Rose—pure love

Strawberry powder—softness and devotion

Sugar—attraction and sweetening

1. Place the bottle into the canvas bag. Hold the bag closed with one hand. Through the bag, carefully use the hammer to hit the bottle until it breaks. You want the pieces to be large enough that they can be glued together, so don't go overboard. While wearing gloves or carefully minding the sharp glass, remove the pieces from the bag.

2. Wearing gloves, mix the epoxy and gold powder together in small batches, as it dries quickly. Use the craft sticks to apply a generous amount of glue to the edge of the broken pieces, then carefully press them back together. Continue until the bottle is reconstituted.

3. After the glue dries, fill the heart bottle with love crystals, botanicals, and symbols from the list above.

4. Hold the bottle to your heart and imagine a bright green light emanating from it. This light fills your chest and surrounds your heart with loving, healing energy. Repeat this ritual whenever you need it.

CHAPTER NINE

Spells for Your Home

• • • • • • • • • • • • • • • • • •

The home is the birthplace of magic and witches. The practices of witchcraft were originally employed by heads of households to keep their families safe and healthy, to protect their homes from evil, and to protect their possessions from greed. Much of the home magic we practice today is the same, even if the ingredients and incantations have changed. The spells in this chapter can also help you find and keep a home, set boundaries with nosy neighbors, and usher positive energy into the homestead and all who reside there.

Housewitching Gift

This jar can be given as a gift when someone moves into a new home. It has everything necessary to cleanse and clear the house of negative energy or malicious entities. This spell adds an aura of protection to the home and a wish of happiness and harmony for the family.

Lighter or matches

Vanilla incense

Large mason jar

4 or 5 small plastic bags

Salt or Witch's Salt (page 88)

Green Money Rice (page 52)

2-ounce spray bottle

Moon Water (page 118)

Red embroidery thread and needle

Disposable gloves

9 whole dried chile peppers

4 black tourmaline crystals

4 rose quartz crystals

4 white tea lights

Pack of matches (for the jar)

Paper and pen (or type and print)

Herb bundle for burning made of rosemary, mugwort, or sage*

Gift bow with adhesive or glue

1. Light a stick of vanilla incense to bring in warm, happy vibes. Use the smoke from the incense to cleanse the jar and all your tools and ingredients.

2. Fill three of the small bags with Witch's Salt (or regular salt) and Green Money Rice, then place them in the jar.

3. Fill a 2-ounce (travel size) spray bottle with Moon Water and place it in the jar.

4. Thread a 9-inch length of embroidery thread through the needle. Tie a big knot at the end of the thread.

5. Next, you'll be using chile peppers, so gloves are recommended. String nine chile peppers through the widest part near the stem. Tie a loop at the other end of the thread and hang on the outside of the jar. Alternatively, you can place the string of peppers into a plastic bag and place it in the jar.

6. Put the four black tourmaline crystals into a bag to protect them, because black tourmaline is a bit fragile. The rose quartz can stay loose. Place the crystals in the jar.

7. Add the tea lights and the pack of matches to the jar, followed by the herb bundle.

8. Handwrite (or type and print) a letter with your wishes for them in their new home and instructions for how to use the items in the jar:

   Crystals—At the four corners of the house, place one of each stone and burn a candle for protection and harmony.

   Herb bundle—Light by the front door and take through every room of the house. Then circle back to the front. Open the door to release the smoke and the energy it's cleared.

   Pepper string—Hang the peppers in your kitchen for protection and passion.

9. Arrange all the items in the jar, replace the lid, and stick your bow on top.

*See the Be Respectful When Practicing Spell Work sidebar on page 18 for guidance on the use of sage.

Home Sweet Home

Whether you're looking to buy or rent, this jar can help you attract the perfect home for you and your family. Use this spell to not only clarify what you need from a new home, but also sweeten the dispositions of realtors and landlords so they'll be agreeable to your offers and applications.

Paper and pen

4 bay leaves, divided

Business card for realtor (optional)

Comfrey root (optional)

Square jar

4 pieces money/ currency

Sugar

Small toy house

Map of desired neighborhood

1. Write out your wish list for a new home. Include your preferences for size, cost, special features, etc. Allow yourself to fantasize, but try to keep it realistic. At the bottom of the paper write "By (date) I will find this home, or something even better" and sign it.

2. On top of your wish list, place three of the bay leaves. If you have a realtor, add their business card. If you're moving out of town, add a pinch of comfrey root. Then fold the items into the paper by folding it in half toward you four times. Place it in the jar.

3. Add the money and say your rent or mortgage budget out loud.

4. Fill the jar half full with sugar.

5. Place the little house in the sugar. Next to it, place a bay leaf so it stands up in the sugar and looks like a tree.

6. Cut a square out of your map that shows your desired neighborhood or the city you're moving to. Place it in the sugar so it stands up behind the house, like a backdrop.

7. Place the jar near the door of your current residence and give it a kiss every time you leave.

The Landlord's Game

Did you know that Monopoly was based on a board game called The Landlord's Game? The original game was created to teach about the dangers of property greed among individuals and corporations. The game we know today is quite the opposite, as cutthroat monopolist values make for more competitive play. This jar combines the pieces from Monopoly and the egalitarian goals of The Landlord's Game to ensure fairness and equity when dealing with landlords. Choose from the suggested game pieces to personalize this spell for your situation. This spell is best done on a Thursday, the day of money and stability.

The following Monopoly pieces:

- 1 bill of each denomination
- 1 property card
- 1 railroad card
- 1 Get Out of Jail Free card
- 5–10 plastic houses or hotels

Black or brown marker

Copy of your lease

Mason jar with lid

Salt

Valerian root

Brown or black candle

Lighter or matches

SUGGESTED MONOPOLY PIECES

Battleship—if anyone in the home is in the military or is a veteran

Car—if you have motorized vehicles

Hat—if you are the head of the household

Scottie dog—if you have pets

Shoe—if you have no car and walk, bike, or use public transit

Thimble or iron—if you have a home business or are crafty

Wheelbarrow—if you have a garden

1. Lay the bills and cards from the game in front of you. Write your address on the front of the property card to represent your home; then, on the back, write your current landlord's name. At the bottom, sign the card.

CONTINUED →

2. On the back of the railroad card draw a picture of a railroad spike, a classic element in protection spells, to anchor you to your home to help prevent eviction. Sign this as well.

3. Sign your name on the Get Out of Jail Free card.

4. Place the cards on top of your lease and fold them all together 4 times.

5. Place your folded packet in the jar and cover with a thick layer of salt.

6. Next, add a layer of plastic houses or hotels.

7. Sign each of the bills. Crumple each bill and add them on top of the houses. This is to ensure you always have money for rent and your checks are deposited properly.

8. Finally, add the suggested game pieces one at a time. Say what they represent out loud followed by "this is your home."

9. Sprinkle valerian root over the top for added protection and to cool arguments and disagreements.

10. Place the lid on the jar and place the candle to the top of the lid. Light the candle and let it burn all the way down, dripping over the edges of the jar.

11. Repeat the candle ritual every month on the day you pay your rent, and whenever you have a dispute with your landlord.

The Hunger Tamed

Food insecurity plagues many people, causing undue stress and pain for many. Not having enough to eat incites a visceral, instinctual fear in us. In witchcraft, alfalfa helps to protect what's in the pantry and your wallet. Try not to spend too much on this spell—if you're missing any ingredient, simply replace it with something else from your kitchen. Alfalfa, salt, and a grain are the most important ingredients.

Basil

Cinnamon sticks

Cocoa powder or
   chocolate chips

Coffee or tea

Cornmeal

Dried fruit

Nuts and seeds

Oats

Rice

Rosemary

Salt

Sugar

Ceramic or clay jar
   with airtight lid

Dried alfalfa

Adhesive label
   and pen

1. In small handfuls, add the food materials to the jar. If any ingredient is immediately edible, eat a small amount of it as you add it to the jar.

2. Top the jar off with dried alfalfa, then breathe in the aroma.

3. On the label, draw a cornucopia spilling over with food and love, or write your favorite mealtime gratitude prayer. Attach the label to the outside of the jar.

4. Seal the jar and place it in the pantry where you can see it.

5. Bring the jar out at mealtimes or before grocery shopping. To reactivate the spell, recite the prayer or meditate on the image.

Good Boundaries Make Good Neighbors

This spell is the magical antidote to nosy neighbors, solicitors, and anyone else who may drop by unexpectedly with ill intentions. I use it anytime I feel my privacy isn't being respected and every time I move into a new apartment. The primary ingredient, Florida Water, is an eau de parfum originally made in France that features citrus and clove oils. It has become popular in North America as an all-purpose magical cleanser that can be found in witch shops and botánicas. Thanks to the alcohol content, it's also a great cleaner and disinfectant. Craft this spell on a Saturday when the moon is waning.

Black obsidian

16-ounce mason jar with spray nozzle

½ cup Florida Water (see page 144)

Warm water

New cleaning cloth

1. Place the black obsidian in the jar. Obsidian is dark volcanic glass and helps magically block prying eyes from seeing inside.

2. Pour the Florida Water on top of the obsidian. Florida Water removes the energy of those who are already struggling to mind their business. The cloves in Florida Water also clear away gossip and trash talk.

3. Pour warm water into the jar, filling it almost to the top.

4. Beginning at the back of the house and working toward the front door, use the cloth dipped in the solution to clean every window. Imagine the outsides of the windows as striking slabs of obsidian, blocking the eyes of others.

5. Dump the window wash outside when you're finished or when it gets so dirty that the solution is opaque.

Rainbow Connection Witch Ball

Throughout history, many people have believed that seeing a rainbow meant that you were not alone. It is believed to be a reminder of God, the universe, or another spiritual presence. This witch ball harnesses that energy to help you feel happy and comfortable at home, even when you feel alone. Craft this spell on a sunny day.

Dried orris (iris) root

Hanging clear, empty glass or plastic ball

Salt

Small opalite crystals

Small rainbow moonstone crystals

Small rainbow obsidian crystals

Hanging suncatcher or prism

Rainbow ribbon

Hook or nail for hanging (optional)

1. Turn off all electronics, music, and sounds that you might use to make the house feel fuller. Bring your materials and tools to a west-facing window. Open the window to let the breeze roll in.

2. Sprinkle dried orris root into the ball. This root comes from the blue iris, which was named after the Greek goddess of the rainbow. She bridged the communication gap between humans and the divine.

3. Next, add a pinch of salt for protection and to cleanse away any feelings of unease or anxiety.

4. Add the crystals one at a time.

   Opalite—helps dissolve feelings of hopelessness

   Rainbow moonstone—reassures anyone who feels lonely or lost and protects from negative energy in moments of vulnerability

   Rainbow obsidian—reminds us that there is light at the end of the tunnel, and darkness is never absolute

5. Hang the suncatcher or prism inside the ball so it rests above the crystals. Pull the string out through the opening of the ball, then close up the ball to keep the string in place. Tie a 7-inch length of rainbow ribbon to the ball and make a loop. Hang the ball on a nail or hook.

Home Guardian Spirit

Throughout the world, ancient religions and practices have featured spirits and deities who reside in and protect the home. Some are magical creatures such as elves and brownies (Britain), and others are the spirits of ancestors who watch over the family from the afterlife. There were also gods who preside over the home and hearth, such as Bes in ancient Egypt, Kamuy-huci in Japan, and Chantico, worshipped by the Nahuas, Indigenous people of Mexico and Central America. This spell helps you visualize a guardian for your home (to ensure you are practicing conscientiously, review the Be Respectful When Practicing Spell Work sidebar on page 18). To craft this spell, call on the spirit of one of your ancestors, or connect with one of these ancient beings.

Statue or image of your chosen ancestor or spirit

Mason jar

Small table or surface

Tablecloth in favorite colors

SUGGESTED MATERIALS

Baby pictures

Birthstones

Family crest or motto

Family heirlooms

Locks of hair and baby teeth

Photos of ancestors

Spare house key

SUGGESTED BOTANICALS AND CRYSTALS

Aquamarine—soothing stressed parents

Citrine—minimize family conflicts

Lavender—comfort and safety

Motherwort—nurturing and health

Rose petals—positive energy and reverence for the divine

Rose quartz—love and protecting children

Rosemary—remembering ancestors

Sugar—sweetness and softness

1. Place a statue or image of your chosen spirit in the jar.

2. Add any suggested materials, botanicals, and crystals that feel connected to your home or the spirit. If you live with others, invite them to pick something small but important to add to the jar. Then replace the lid of the jar.

3. Choose a small table or surface in the center, or heart, of the home. Add a tablecloth. Place the jar on the tablecloth.

4. Say hello and goodbye to the guardian when you leave and return, to form a connection. Talk to your home guardian on a regular basis, even when it's not visible.

5. If the jar becomes dirty or forgotten, clean and cleanse the jar. Offer food and water every day for as long as it was neglected.

SUGGESTED PRACTICES

- Burn a candle on top of the jar every week.

- Keep your home guardian near family photos and heirlooms to encourage ancestors to visit and offer protection.

- Whenever you have a family meal or celebration, offer a small plate of food to the home guardian. The next day, dispose of it outside for nature to claim.

- If your guardian is an animal, add shed fur or whiskers from family pets. This will help protect your animals, too.

CHAPTER TEN

Spells for Connecting with the Natural World

N ature is the second most important power source a witch can tap, the first being themself, of course, but it is also a trusted friend, mother, creator, and provider. Whether you've got a green thumb or a black one, live in a city or in the woods, or if you observe nature mostly from afar, you can connect with the earth. This chapter will help you see and understand the inherent magic of the planet through exploration, creation, and getting your hands dirty.

Moon Water

Moon water is very simple to make but remarkably versatile. Moon water is the witch's version of holy water, meaning it's simple water from the earth that has been blessed for use in all sorts of spiritual situations. In this case, the spiritual power comes from the full moon and your own innate magic. Begin this spell on the night of the full moon and be prepared to collect it before the sun rises.

Lighter or matches	Spring water	Sea salt (optional)
Jasmine incense	1 tablespoon lemon juice	Moonstone (optional)
Clear glass bottle with airtight cap		

1. On the night of the full moon, gather your materials and head outside or to a window with moonlight shining in.

2. Light the jasmine incense and use the smoke to cleanse the jar and yourself.

3. Fill the bottle with the spring water, then add the lemon juice. If you don't plan to drink it, you can also add a tablespoon of sea salt. Lemon juice keeps the water from going flat or growing mold, and lemon is also a sacred lunar plant.

4. Replace the cap and set the moonstone on top of the bottle (**not** in the water).

5. Infuse the water with intentions by holding the bottle and imagining glowing light pouring out of your heart and through your hands.

6. Remain outside or at the window until the incense burns down, praying or speaking to the moon.

7. Bring the Moon Water inside before the sun rises. Use it right away or keep it in the refrigerator for up to a month.

Summertime Sadness Jar

Every season is beautiful, and I feel fortunate to live in a place that gets all of them—but winter can be a serious challenge. It is incredibly common for people to get sad, depressed,* irritable, and fatigued in the winter when days are gray and sunless. This jar brings sunlight and warmth back into your days, even when they're dark and cold. Craft this jar in the middle of the day on Sunday.

Pink salt

16-ounce clear mason jar

3 bay leaves

St. John's wort flowers

Sunflower petals or seeds

Sunstone

Yellow calcite crystal

White Howlite crystal

Solar light mason jar lid with attached fairy lights

1. Start by clearing the blues away. Add a ½-inch layer of pink salt to the jar.

2. Add the bay leaves. Then add small handfuls of St. John's wort and sunflower petals or seeds.

3. Add the crystals one at a time, taking a moment to meditate on the energy they provide for your spell. Sunstone helps increase your energy and encourages you to manifest your dreams. Yellow calcite clears stagnant energy and can bring you out of a rut. Wintery-looking Howlite exudes the energy of compassion and softness.

4. Arrange the fairy lights within the jar, then affix the solar light lid.

5. Place the jar in a window to charge. Then turn it on and bask in the glow of solar energy. Imagine sunny places, warm experiences, and bright days full of life.

*If you feel so depressed it begins to interfere with your life or health, please reach out to a doctor or therapist. Seasonal Affective Disorder is very serious, and any light therapy treatment should take place under the care of a professional. Magic works best for healing when used in tandem with science.

Sweet Beginnings and Endings

This spell creates a tasty syrup that can be added to pancakes or waffles, but the botanicals included make it much more than a sweet treat. Maple syrup is made very early in the spring, when snow is still on the ground but plants are starting to come to life. Autumn is the time when the earth prepares for the darkness of winter. This magical syrup helps you harness the hopeful and bright energy of the spring and combines it with the shadowy approach of winter.

Salt water

16-ounce bottle with airtight lid or pouring spout

Saucepan

16 ounces maple syrup

3 cinnamon sticks

1 broken nutmeg seed

6 cardamom pods

3 cloves

Stirring spoon

Strainer

16-ounce glass measuring cup with spout

1. Use salt water to clean your bottle and the tools you'll be using, as well as the space around the stove where you're working.

2. In a saucepan over medium heat, bring the maple syrup to a simmer.

3. Add the cinnamon, nutmeg seed, cardamom pods, and cloves. Simmer on medium-low for 6 to 12 minutes, stirring frequently.

4. Remove from the burner and let it sit for 12 minutes.

5. Place the strainer over the measuring cup. Strain out the spices and discard them.

6. When the syrup has cooled, pour it into the bottle. As you pour, imagine the dark amber of the syrup begins to glow with light. That light is filled with luck, optimism, love, and magic.

7. Call the image of the light to mind whenever you use the syrup. Allow it to fill you with its warm magic as you eat.

As Above, So Below

You might have heard the above phrase before. It's popular in witch-craft, hermeticism, and many new age and magical religions. It stems from a paraphrased excerpt of an ancient Arabic text called the Emerald Tablet. The translation is different depending on who you ask, but the original verse was *"That which is above is from that which is below, and that which is below is from that which is above."* Everything that makes up the earth, humanity, the universe—it's all connected, all the same.

This spell is a meditation on this sentiment, connecting you with the earth in profound and unexpected ways. "As above, so below" is illustrated in the tarot on the Magician card, where we see the Magician pointing to the sky and the earth and working with representations of the four elements in front of them. This card represents potential and willpower, but also a connection to all the magic both above and below. Execute this spell on a clear day when you can see the sky.

4 test tubes with caps

Marker

Lighter or matches

Frankincense incense

Magician tarot card or printout

Journal and pen

SUGGESTED ELEMENTAL MATERIALS

Air—feathers, dandelion seeds

Earth—dirt, salt, botanicals

Fire—dried chiles, volcanic stones

Water—snow, rain, river or ocean water

1. On a clear day, venture outside with your test tubes and marker. Collect a representation for each element using the suggestions as guidance. Label each tube with the alchemical symbol for its corresponding element:

CONTINUED→

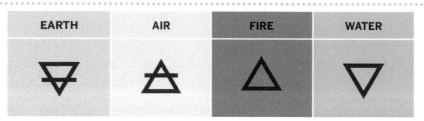

EARTH	AIR	FIRE	WATER

2. Bring the test tubes home and light a stick of frankincense to acknowledge the invisible fifth element of spirit/aether/void.

3. Sit down with the Magician card in front of you. Inspect each vial and the element inside.

4. In your journal, ponder the nature of the elements and what they mean to you. Refer to the basic meanings on page 32, but dig deeper into what these materials mean to you. Where else can you find this element on earth? Where can you find this element outside of our atmosphere, in the cosmos? Write these thoughts as if you were the Magician on the tarot card, wielding elemental magic to manifest a beautiful future. What role does each element play?

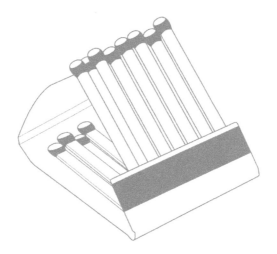

Seven of Pentacles Compost "Tea"

Composting is a fantastic, eco-friendly endeavor. I've even heard witches compare their compost bin to a cauldron where they brew up earth magic. Think of this as the "city witch" version—compost tea. It has nutrients for your plants or garden, and it gives a second life to your waste before it hits the landfill. Note that this "tea" is not to be consumed by people or animals—just plants.

Seven of Pentacles tarot card or printout

Clear packing tape

Large mason jar with airtight lid

Eggshells

Coffee grounds

Used tea bags

Banana peels

Moon Water (with no salt included)

Strainer

Watering can

Fresh water

1. Start by observing your Seven of Pentacles. Take in the scene depicted on the card. This card is about watching the garden, an investment in your future, grow. It's also about sustainability and personal responsibility.

2. Covering it with clear tape, adhere the image onto the jar. Place the empty jar on the kitchen counter.

3. For the next seven days, place any of your eggshells, coffee grounds, tea bags, and banana peels into the jar. At the end of the week, fill the jar with Moon Water and replace the lid.

4. Leave the jar to sit for seven days. On each day, look at the jar and say, "My dedication to sustainability and growth will pay off for me *and* the planet."

5. Strain the solid material out of the liquid and discard the solids.

6. Add the water mixture to a watering can with an equal amount of fresh water. Use it to water your plants and garden.

Walk in the Woods Oil

It has been proven time and time again that both spending time in nature and bringing nature into your living space have life-changing positive effects. Nature can positively impact your mood, mental clarity, energy levels, and just overall well-being. Depending on where you live, it may be difficult to immerse yourself in nature. This blend mimics the smell of a forest path on a beautiful day so anyone can enjoy the benefits of a close relationship with the planet.

Funnel

Droppers

3 drops bergamot essential oil

3 drops cedarwood essential oil (3 drops)

1 drop geranium essential oil

3 drops juniper or pine essential oil

3 drops patchouli essential oil

2 drops sweetgrass essential oil

1 drop vanilla essential oil

1 teaspoon light olive oil

15- or 20-milliliter amber or green bottle

1. Using a funnel and droppers, add the essential oils and olive oil to the bottle. Leave space at the top so you can add more essential oil.

2. Replace the cap and give it a good shake. Give it a few minutes to settle, then close your eyes and sniff the mixture. Imagine the type of forest that would smell this way. See the trees, feel the earth beneath your feet, smell the sweetgrass and geraniums in a nearby meadow.

3. Add more essential oils to create a unique aroma. When the smell is to your liking, cap the bottle and keep it out of sunlight.

4. Smell this oil to help you connect to nature even when you're surrounded by concrete. You can also wear it as a perfume during earth element spells and rituals or diffuse the oil in your home when you need the cleansing fragrance of the outdoors.

Dirty Witch

You don't have to spend a lot of money on special tools, herbs, powders, or spell ingredients to work earth magic. Dirt can be used in many different spells, and when and where you collect it can help power specific intentions. This isn't a spell; this is a field trip. Explore these different kinds of magical earth and collect some for your future spells.

Small airtight bottles or jars

Spoon

Adhesive labels

Pen

Offerings

SUGGESTED SOURCES OF DIRT

Bank dirt—obtaining or saving money, approval for loans and financing, or freedom from debt

Beach sand— peace, love, water element, stability through change, transformation

Courthouse dirt—justice in a particular legal issue or in general

Crossroads dirt— opening roads, releasing spells to the universe, decision-making, guidance

Graveyard dirt—all manner of spiritual assistance, hexing or cursing, speaking with the dead

Home dirt— connection to the person who lives there and the property itself

1. Bring your containers and materials to your selected location. If you're collecting dirt from a gravesite, see the specific notes on the next page.

2. Collect your dirt and label your containers.

3. Always leave an offering behind as payment.

4. Use the dirt in small increments—you don't need much. Sprinkle it onto your altar, on candles, or add it to spell jars and bottles.

CONTINUED➜

Notes on graveyard dirt: No matter where you collect your dirt, it's customary to leave something behind as payment or gratitude. Nowhere is this more important than at the graveyard. You can collect dirt from the cemetery gates for protection and boundaries. The customary offering is coins—preferably silver. The amounts vary, but choose a magical or significant number, or one of each denomination. Another traditional offering is the favorite types of alcohol or tobacco of the deceased. You can also play their favorite song, bring their favorite foods, and clean up their grave area.

When you take dirt from any specific grave, you are basically employing that spirit, or their energy, in your spell work. So, if you want justice, find the grave of a judge. If you want success, visit the grave of a wealthy person. If you want to connect with ancestors, collect dirt from their graves.

Take a moment to talk to the spirit and explain what you want and why. If you feel anything scary or unpleasant, move on. If everything seems okay, take a small amount and place it in a jar. Label it with their name, birth and death dates, and vocation.

Faerrarium

To many people, faeries are fictional beings from children's stories. But those stories originated in places where faeries and other nature spirits are as real as you and I. By building a beautiful garden just for them, this spell jar will help you form a spiritual connection with these nature spirits. If don't have a green thumb, you can build a craft terrarium—which isn't as alive, but still features natural items and makes them feel at home. For a craft terrarium, use a decorative glass container with an open side, preserved mosses, and arid botanicals such as succulents and air plants.

Large, clear, wide-mouth glass container with airtight lid

Small pebbles

Mesh

Sphagnum moss

Activated charcoal

Springtails (optional)

Moist potting soil

Natural rocks

Moss

Miniature orchids

Bark

Twigs

Acorn caps

Long paintbrush

Long tweezers

Clay or ceramic faerie decor (e.g., small house or door, chairs, small toadstools, cups)

Spray bottle with filtered water

Paper towel

SUGGESTED CRYSTALS AND BOTANICALS

Clear quartz—creates pure magic

Faerie quartz—facilitates magical vision

Moss agate—helps plants grow, especially moss

Petrified wood—invokes ancient magic and wisdom

Prehnite—communicates with and grabs the attention of faeries and nature spirits

Tree agate—connects the terrarium to all the trees and plants on earth

CONTINUED →

1. Layer your ingredients. Start with 2 inches of pebbles, then add a piece of mesh cut to be the same size and shape as the jar, sphagnum moss, activated charcoal, springtails, another mesh layer, moist potting soil, rocks, and moss.

2. After you have laid down your base layer, add the magical décor of your choice—orchids, bark, twigs, more rocks, and acorn caps.

3. Use the paintbrush and tweezers to move items around and make it look like a miniature natural landscape. Create hills, trees, and other natural elements.

4. Add faerie decor, crystals, and any other magical items you think would appease the spirits of nature.

5. Give your garden a good spray down with filtered water and let it soak in. Use a paper towel to wipe off the inside of the jar so it's clear.

6. Finally, place the lid on the jar and leave it. This is a self-sustaining ecosystem. You can open the jar from time to time to check for mold, but leave it closed most of the time.

SUGGESTED PRACTICES

- Make music using bells and wind chimes to invite faeries to the terrarium.

- Fill one of the acorn caps with water as a peace offering.

- If you have sweets or dessert, leave a small amount next to the jar for the faeries, and dispose of it in the garden the next day for nature to claim.

- To get the attention of the spirits of nature, add objects that sparkle and shine.

For more thorough guidelines on how to create a living terrarium, visit the Resources section (page 147).

CHAPTER ELEVEN

Spells for Navigating Daily Life

● ● ● ● ● ● ● ● ● ● ● ● ● ● ●

No matter what life throws at you, magic is there to block it, catch it, or slow it down. In happy times, we can create celebratory spell jars. Using the same materials, we can create talismans, wards, and containers for grief for when things get tough. These everyday spells will help you stay healthy, celebrate life, get justice, and make your dreams come true.

The Witch's Court

Whether you're going to court as a defendant or a lawyer, this spell bottle can help your case run smoothly. Craft this spell to lead the jury or judge toward seeing the truth and to prevent trash talk or misinformation being shared in the courtroom. Craft this jar on the Sunday before your court date.

Small bottle with a cork (no metal)

Pinch courthouse dirt

Pinch brown sugar

Red jasper and lapis lazuli stones

Deer's tongue or slippery elm

3 whole cloves or clove powder

Calendula petals

Lighter or matches

Brown chime candle

1. In the bottle, combine courthouse dirt and brown sugar.

2. If there will be a jury, add 12 lapis lazuli or red jasper stones. Lapis lazuli promotes truth and positive communication, and red jasper supports victory and justice. If there will only be a judge and no jury, add one piece of each.

3. Add a pinch of deer's tongue or slippery elm for the power of convincing communication. Add the whole cloves or a pinch of clove powder to keep gossip and rumors out of the courtroom. Finally, add a pinch of calendula petals for victory and respect.

4. Replace the cork and melt brown candle wax over the top to help ensure you'll be back home soon.

5. Carry the spell into court as inconspicuously as possible. For example, tuck it into a secret pocket or your right sock.

6. As you enter the courthouse, say "*The judge [or the jury] will see that I am [or my client is] innocent [or, that the defendant is guilty].*"

7. If you win, deconstruct the bottle and bury the contents outside. If you lose, throw the bottle away before leaving the courthouse.

Put a Cork in It

Fake news spreads pretty fast these days, especially on the Internet. This powder can be used to stop the spread of lies and misinformation and to prevent gossip queens and bullies from saying your name.

Sea salt	Mortar and pestle	Lighter
Cloves	Small black tourmaline crystal	1 sheet aluminum foil
Slippery elm		Bottle with cork (optional: ultraviolet glass)
Eggshells	Paper and a green pen	

1. Add equal parts salt, cloves, slippery elm, and eggshells to the mortar and pestle, along with a small black tourmaline.

2. Break up the crystal and grind all the ingredients together into a powder. Set this mixture aside.

3. Think of any rumors or gossipers that you want to put a stop to. Gather a sheet of paper, a green pen, a lighter, and some foil. On one side of the paper, write the rumors and lies. On the other side, write the name of the offender nine times backwards. Light the paper on fire and drop it onto the foil. Let it burn to ash.

4. Mix the ashes with your powder and add the mixture to your bottle.

5. Say the following spell while you cork the bottle:

   No more lies to tell,
   No more trash to talk,
   Put a cork in it and take a walk!

6. After interactions with the gossip queen, sprinkle the powder around you. You can also sprinkle it onto the offender's shoes, or onto your phone to address online rumors.

Rest Bottle

Rest is important to our health, but it doesn't come naturally to us these days. It's common to push ourselves, hustle harder, and try to do it all even though we know we'll burn out eventually. This bottle helps prevent burnout by allowing you to get the most out of moments of rest and relaxation. Craft this bottle in your bedroom during the new moon, when people tend to sleep the best.

Bottle or jar with a metal lid (optional: cobalt blue glass)

Chamomile

Lavender

Poppy seeds

Mugwort

Howlite crystal

Citrine

Celestite

Selenite

Lighter or matches

White or dark blue candle

1. Gather your materials on a dresser or table in your bedroom.

2. Fill the jar to the top with equal amounts of chamomile, lavender, poppy seeds, and mugwort. Chamomile promotes waking up rested, and lavender eases anxiety and racing thoughts. Poppy seeds remind us to slow down and rest, and mugwort provides spiritual dream protection.

3. Add the crystals one at a time, pausing to touch them to your third eye before they go in the jar. Start with white Howlite, which quiets the mind so you can easily drift off. Sleep peacefully with the help of citrine, which offers protection from nightmares, and celestite, which promotes continuous sleep. Selenite also prevents disruption from changing moon phases and snoring. Once all the crystals are nestled safely in the embrace of the herbs, cap the jar. Use a flame to melt the bottom of a white or dark blue candle so you can stick it on top of the container.

4. Place the jar on the nightstand next to your bed and light the candle. Lie down and rest for at least 20 minutes, but don't fall asleep with the candle lit.

5. When you need help enjoying your rest, light the candle and think of yourself like those crystals, nestled safely in the soft embrace of the earth. Repeat this spell during the full moon phases and anytime you're struggling to sleep.

Birthday Star Jar

Happy Birthday! This giftable jar celebrates the day a special person came into the world. This jar will need some customization and research on your part—look up your friend's birthstone and the colors, incense, and symbols associated with it. Find their birth chart on a site such as Astro-Charts.com and print it out. Look online or in a witch shop for zodiac incense, or buy a scent associated with their sign. Get a small gift like a necklace, keychain, charm, or piece of art with their birthstone, or their sign's symbol or constellation.

Birthday candles in the color associated with their zodiac

Transparent glass mason jar, clear or in the elemental color associated with their zodiac

Elemental treat (e.g., saltwater taffy for water signs, nuts for earth signs, hot candy for fire, dried fruit for air)

Incense associated with their zodiac

Physical representations of their zodiac

Printout of their birth chart

Their birthstone (monthly or zodiac)

Picture of the person having a birthday (baby pictures are ideal)

Pen

Glue or tape

Glass markers or paint (optional)

Ribbon or bow in the color associated with their zodiac

1. Hold birthday candles in your hands and close your eyes. Think of the things you love about your friend and all the wishes you have for their future. Hold them up to your mouth and whisper "My love for you will help you make all your wishes come true."

2. Arrange the treats and gifts in the jar. Roll up or fold the birth chart to fit.

3. On the back of your friend's photo, write their full name and birthday, your nickname for them, and three things you love about them. Affix it to the jar with glue or tape. If you like, you can use glass markers or paint to decorate the jar.

4. Sing "Happy Birthday" into the jar to fill it with love. You can also sing a special song that reminds you of your friend.

5. Cap the jar, add a bow or ribbon, and remind your friend how much you love them when you gift it to them.

Sweet Success

Tension in the office can make every day feel sour and bitter. Problematic co-workers or overwhelming demands can feel utterly out of our control. This incognito spell jar brings a little sweetness, relaxation, truth, and positivity to you and all your co-workers—and not just because it's full of candy.

Blue Pen	Black pen	Salt
Clear candy jar	Ground cloves	Hot glue
Light blue felt	Dried lavender, echinacea, basil, and sage	Candies
Company business card		

1. Use the blue pen to trace the shape of the bottom of the jar onto two pieces of light blue felt.

2. Think of what is causing discord in the office. On the business card, write the names of the co-workers or situations with a blue pen. Then cross them out with black.

3. Place the card in the center of one of the pieces of felt. One at a time, sprinkle each dried herb in a circle around the business card. Take a pinch of salt and sprinkle it over the card itself.

4. Use hot glue to stick the two pieces of felt together, taking care not to leave any gaps or holes that could let your ingredients fall out.

5. Glue the felt packet to the bottom of the jar. Fill the jar with candy and offer a piece to everyone in the office. This spell will encourage everyone to keep the peace.

Witchy Climate Cover

Did you know there are crystals for every season, day of the week, climate, and even every natural disaster? These ancient wonders have inhabited the planet for hundreds of thousands of years and have witnessed many varieties of climates and weather. Some were even forged in erupting volcanoes (lava), cracking lightning (fulgurite), and fiery collisions between the earth and nearby celestial bodies (meteorite). Crystals can be remarkable talismans for protection and safety in tempestuous times. Customize your spell to harness their power for protecting yourself or your home. Choose crystals that apply to the weather where you are (or where you're going). Work this magic near an open window on a clear, beautiful day.

MATERIALS FOR HOME USE

Square glass jar

Dirt from your property

MATERIALS FOR PERSONAL USE

Small bottle

Strand of hair

SUGGESTED CRYSTALS

Aquamarine—flood and rain protection

Celestite—divine protection and clear skies

Citrine—heat wave protection and sunny days

Desert Rose selenite crystal—sandstorm and wind protection

Lava stone—volcano and earthquake protection

Meteorite/Gibeon meteorite dust—violent and unpredictable weather protection

Petrified wood—forest fire protection and keeping your home intact

Pietersite—hurricane, tornado, tempest protection

CONTINUED ➜

Smoky quartz— human error, smoke, and fog protection

Snow quartz—snow, sleet, cold, and hail protection

Sodalite or fulgurite—lightning and electrical storm protection

1. Add the property dirt or strand of hair to your container, linking the spell to you.

2. Add the crystals of your choice, one at a time, pausing to focus on the powers of each one. Imagine the weather suddenly clearing up—tornadoes losing momentum, fires extinguished by gentle rain, clouds parting.

3. Cap the container. Leave it near your entranceway, mudroom, or storm cellar.

4. When the weather starts to change, bring your container outside if it is safe to do so. Let the spell experience the weather firsthand. Anoint it with rainwater, snow, or rushing winds.

5. The home jar should be returned to its safe place, and a personal bottle should be kept in your purse, pocket, or shoes until it's needed again.

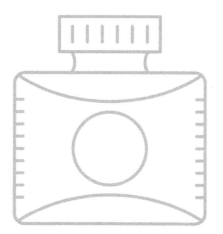

Pandora's Jar of Hope

When the death, sickness, and pain left Pandora's jar, all that remained inside was hope. Grief and loss can make us lose hope for the future. We can feel like we are being torn apart. Craft this memorial jar to soothe the pain of grief, and cast a spell of hope on you, your home, and those you've lost.

Lidded jar of your choice

Graveyard dirt

Flower from their grave

MATERIALS OF REMEMBRANCE

Heirloom or item they owned

Item that represents your relationship with them

Personal letter

Photo of the deceased or their family

Symbols of their religion

Candles in their favorite color (or white candles)

Indulgences of theirs (e.g., chocolate, liquor, coffee, lottery tickets)

SUGGESTED HERBS OF REMEMBRANCE

Bay leaves—blessings for young boys

Bittersweet flowers or berries—contentious relationship full of love

Calendula/marigold—happiness in the afterworld

Catnip, alfalfa, oregano, or birdseed—pet cats, rabbits, dogs, or birds

Copal—enticing their spirit to visit

Hemp—spirit protection

Lilies—saying goodbye

Motherwort—blessings for moms and nurturers

Mugwort—spiritual protection

Mullein—lighting the way for spirits

Myrrh—rebirth and reincarnation

Oak leaves or bark—blessings for ancestors

Rosemary—remembrance

Sage—cleansing negativity

Violets—blessings for young girls

CONTINUED →

Pandora's Jar of Hope CONTINUED

SUGGESTED CRYSTALS OF REMEMBRANCE

Angelite and celestite—to guide your loved one through the afterlife

Animal agates

Apache tear obsidian— comfort during moments of grief

Bloodstone—family, blood, and ancestors

Garnet—hope for the future

Lepidolite—keeping depression and hopelessness at bay

Rose quartz— unconditional love

1. As you begin this spell, conjure up memories of your loved one.

2. Open your chosen container and add a sprinkle of graveyard dirt. If possible, add a flower from their grave.

3. Next, add the items that remind you of your loved one. Include any personal items, including photos, letters, symbols, and heirlooms. Around the items, place the candles.

4. Choose any herbs or crystals of remembrance that you feel are connected with your loved one and add them to the container.

5. Close the container and place it somewhere special. As time goes on, surround your jar with photos of living family members and friends, so the deceased knows they are still a part of your story. Open the jar regularly and share your hopes and dreams with them.

SUGGESTED PRACTICES

- Write letters to your loved one and place them in the jar.

- Create a memorial altar space where you burn candles and incense in honor of the deceased.

- On Halloween, All Saints' Day, or All Souls' Day, encourage them to visit for the night. Burn copal incense, place fresh marigolds, and offer sweet foods and celebratory drinks.

GLOSSARY

African diasporic religions: African traditional religions are those that were or are practiced in Africa by various African societies, and diasporic religions are those that were created/practiced in the Americas after the transatlantic slave trade. These include Hoodoo, Haitian vodou, New Orleans voodoo, Brazilian candomblé, Cuban Lucumi (Santeria), and Jamaican Rastafarianism, among others.

Botanicals: plant parts, extracts, and preparation. It is also often used interchangeably with "plants" or "herbs" as a catchall.

Carrier oil: a base oil, usually odorless, that dilutes essential oils and helps "carry" them into your body. Olive, sweet almond, sunflower, and coconut are examples of carrier oils.

Embodiment (embody): the act of taking an energy into your body by identifying with it, and then expressing that energy in a physical way.

Florida Water: an eau de parfum or eau de toilette that was considered gender neutral. Its main scents are citrus (sweet orange) and clove. The Murray & Lanman brand has been produced since 1808 and is the most common version used in Hoodoo and magic. Its name is a reference to the mythical Fountain of Youth discovered in Florida by Ponce de Leon. It's used in Hoodoo and witchcraft for spiritual cleansing and protection.

Grimoire: a book of magic. There are multiple names for a witch's personal book of magic, including Book of Shadows, Book of Life, or simply Spell Book. It can contain spells, recipes, ingredients, and other reference materials or serve as a magical journal or diary that chronicles your spiritual journey.

Manifestation (manifest): using magic to make something materialize, or to bring about an intended result. For example, you can manifest money or a new job.

Meditation: sitting quietly, clearing your mind, connecting to spiritual energy or contemplating something specific from a spiritual perspective.

Mythology: a sacred story from the beginnings of a culture or civilization that outlines their spiritual and religious beliefs. It does not specifically mean it is a fictional story. Most myths are so old there is no way to confirm whether they really happened.

Photosensitive: to have chemical, electrical, or physical response to light—often in a negative way. Skin can be photosensitive, as can essential oils and crystals. In magic, anything photosensitive should be kept out of direct sunlight at risk of harming it; and in the case of essential oils, some can make your skin photosensitive, which means they can cause burns—undiluted lavender essential oil has this effect.

Spell: an act of spiritual belief or devotion using magical energy. Spells can be used to contact the divine (like a prayer) or to release one's innate magical power— or both.

Tarot cards: a seventy-eight-card system of divination and self-discovery. When it was created sometime in fifteenth-century Italy it was simply a card game. There are many versions of tarot decks, but they all use the same structure and overall meanings. Oracle cards are also used for divination, but their structure is determined by the creator.

Terrarium: a glass enclosure filled with soil, plants, and sometimes living creatures. A closed terrarium is a self-sustaining little ecosystem, and an open terrarium requires regular maintenance like other houseplants. Craft terraria are not living and are made with artificial decorations.

Witch: a person who practices witchcraft. Not all magical practice is witchcraft, however, and others may use words like healer, shaman, priestess, or simply practitioner.

RESOURCES

Blackthorn, Amy. *Blackthorn's Botanical Magic: The Green Witch's Guide to Essential Oils for Spellcraft, Ritual & Healing*. Newburyport, MA: Weiser Books, 2018.

Dempsey, Cindy. "Fordite's History: From Paint to Precious Gem." Fordite .com. Accessed December 6, 2019. Fordite.com/history.

Dorsey, Lilith. *Voodoo and African Traditional Religion*. New Orleans: Warlock Press, 2021.

Eason, Cassandra. *The Complete Crystal Handbook: Your Guide to More Than 500 Crystals*. New York: Sterling Publishing Company, Inc., 2010.

Esselmont, Brigit. *The Ultimate Guide to Tarot Card Meanings*. Scotts Valley: CreateSpace Independent Publishing Platform, 2017.

Gottesdiener, Sarah Faith. *The Moon Book: Lunar Magic to Change Your Life*. New York: St. Martin's Essentials, 2020.

Kolisch, Niki. "How to Make Your Own Bottle Garden—DIY Closed Terrarium." SuperMoss. December 23, 2021. SuperMoss.com/how -to-make-your-own-bottle-garden-diy-closed-terrarium.

Vanderbeck, Paige. *The Fat Feminist Witch Podcast*. Podcast audio. TheFatFeministWitch.com.

———. *Green Witchcraft: A Practical Guide to Discovering the Magic of Plants, Herbs, Crystals, and Beyond*. Emeryville, CA: Rockridge Press, 2020.

———. *Witchcraft for Emotional Wisdom: Spells, Rituals, and Remedies for Healing*. Emeryville, CA: Rockridge Press, 2021.

REFERENCES

Aida, Miss. *Hoodoo Cleansing and Protection Magic: Banish Negative Energy and Ward Off Unpleasant People*. Newburyport, MA: Weiser Books, 2020.

———. *Hoodoo Justice Magic: Spells for Power, Protection and Righteous Vindication*. Newburyport, MA: Weiser Books, 2021.

Basile, Lisa Marie. *Light Magic for Dark Times: More than 100 Spells, Rituals, and Practices for Coping in a Crisis*. Beverly, MA: Fair Winds Press, 2018.

Biali Haas, MD, Susan. "Working With Your Hands Does Wonders for Your Brain." *Psychology Today*. June 21, 2019. PsychologyToday.com/us/blog/prescriptions-life/201906/working-your-hands-does-wonders-your-brain.

Bird, Stephanie Rose. *Sticks, Stones, Roots & Bones: Hoodoo, Mojo & Conjuring with Herbs*. St. Paul, MN: Llewellyn, 2004.

Carmichael, Joe. "Hexagons Are as Close as Science Gets to Magic." *Inverse.com*. February 8, 2016. Inverse.com/article/18926-hexagons-nature-science-sacred-geometry-explainer.

Cuccia, Vanessa. *Crystal Healing and Sacred Pleasure: Awaken Your Sensual Energy Using Crystals and Healing Rituals, One Chakra at a Time*. Beverly, MA: Fair Winds Press, 2018.

Cunningham, Scott. *The Complete Book of Incense, Oils & Brews*. St. Paul, MN: Llewellyn, 1989.

Dorsey, Lilith. *Love Magic: Over 250 Magical Spells and Potions for Getting It, Keeping It, and Making It Last*. Newburyport, MA: Weiser Books, 2016.

———. *Water Magic: Elements of Witchcraft*. Woodbury, MN: Llewellyn, 2020.

Dugan, Ellen. *The Enchanted Cat: Feline Fascinations, Spells and Magick*. Woodbury, MN: Lllewellyn, 2006.

Eaton, Joe, and Ron Sullivan. "Bottle Trees' Lineage Traced to Africa."
SFGATE. May 10, 2009. SFGATE.com/homeandgarden/article/bottle
-trees-lineage-traced-to-Africa-3242847.php.

Fahrun, Mary-Grace. *Italian Folk Magic: Rue's Kitchen Witchery.*
Newburyport, MA: Weiser Books, 2018.

Herstik, Gabriela. *Bewitching the Elements: A Guide to Empowering
Yourself Through Earth, Air, Fire, Water, and Spirit.* New York:
TarcherPerigee, 2020.

Hutcheson, Cory Thomas. *New World Witchery: A Trove of North American
Folk Magic.* Woodbury, MN: Llewellyn, 2021.

Leafar, Elhoim. *The Magical Art of Crafting Charm Bags: 100 Mystical
Formulas for Success, Love, Wealth, and Wellbeing.* Newburyport, MA:
Weiser Books, 2017.

Pamita, Madame. *The Book of Candle Magic: Candle Spell Secrets to
Change Your Life.* Woodbury, MN: Llewellyn, 2020.

Skelcher, Barrie. *Vaseline Glassware.* Atglen, PA: Schiffer, 2007.

Smith, Jacki. *Coventry Magic with Candles, Oils, and Herbs.* San Francisco
Weiser Books, 2011.

Vanderbeck, Paige. *The Grimoire Journal: A Place to Record Spells,
Rituals, Recipes, and More.* Emeryville, CA: Rockridge Press, 2020.

Whitehurst, Tess. *Magical Housekeeping: Simple Charms & Practical Tips
for Creating a Harmonious Home.* Woodbury, MN: Llewellyn, 2010.

———. *The Magic of Flowers: A Guide to Their Metaphysical Uses &
Properties.* Woodbury, MN: Llewellyn, 2013.

Yronwode, Catherine. "Honey Jar and Sugar Box Magic Spells." Lucky
Mojo Curio Co. LuckyMojo.com/honeyjar.html.

INDEX

ABOUT THE AUTHOR

 **Paige Vanderbeck** is the author of *Green Witchcraft*, *The Grimoire Journal*, and *Witchcraft for Emotional Wisdom*. She found witchcraft in the pages of books during the "Wiccan Wave" of the 1990s and, despite being a total Capricorn, has been devoted to the mystical and magical ever since. In 2015, she created *The Fat Feminist Witch Podcast*, a show that aims to make all people feel welcome to and empowered by witchcraft just as they are.

Paige currently watches the full moon from her apartment window in downtown Windsor, Ontario, with two retired street cats who make her laugh every day. Check her out at TheFatFeministWitch.com.

CPSIA information can be obtained
at www.ICGtesting.com
Printed in the USA
JSHW031755100622
26783JS00004B/4